#19

MAESTEG AND TONDU LINES

Vic Mitchell and Keith Smith

MP Middleton Press

Front cover: Once seen widely in the Welsh Valleys, an ex-GWR 0-6-0PT waits at Bridgend to run to Maesteg and beyond on 2nd August 1958. (G.Adams/M.J.Stretton coll.)

Back cover upper: Tondu was at the crossroads of the coal carrying network and shunting coal near its massive signal box on 26th September 1985 was diesel no. 37225. (D.H.Mitchell)

Back cover lower: No. 143606 is waiting to leave Maesteg at 12.24 on 15th October 1992, only two weeks after the line had reopened to passengers after over 20 years of deprivation. (N.Sprinks)

Published October 2011

ISBN 978 1 908174 06 2

© Middleton Press, 2011

Design Deborah Esher

Published by
> *Middleton Press*
> *Easebourne Lane*
> *Midhurst*
> *West Sussex*
> *GU29 9AZ*

Tel: 01730 813169
Fax: 01730 812601
Email: info@middletonpress.co.uk
www.middletonpress.co.uk

Printed in the United Kingdom by Henry Ling Limited, at the Dorset Press, Dorchester, DT1 1HD

CONTENTS

INDEX

BR Diagram for 1951. Not all the halts are shown.

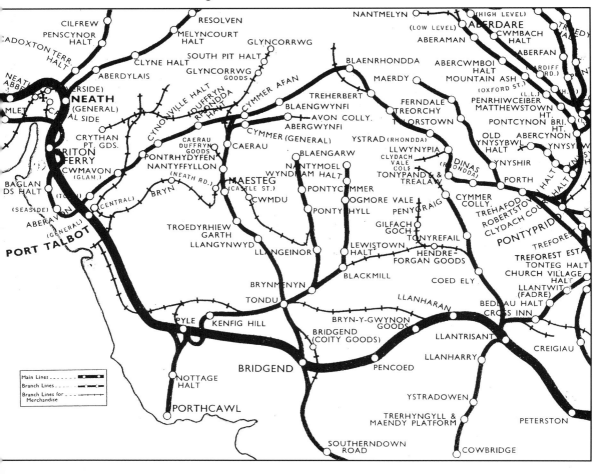

ACKNOWLEDGEMENTS

We are very grateful for the assistance re-ceived from many of those mentioned in the credits also to B.Bennett, P.G.Barnes, A.R.Carder, G.Croughton, S.C.Jenkins, P.J.Kelley, N.Langridge, B.Lewis, D.T.Rowe, Mr D. and Dr S. Salter, S.Vincent, T.Walsh and in particular, our always supportive wives, Barbara Mitchell and Janet Smith.

I. Route diagram showing passenger stations illustrated in this album as solid dots. Their closure dates are in brackets. Only selected collieries are shown. (N.Langridge)

The album section numbers are shown in circles.

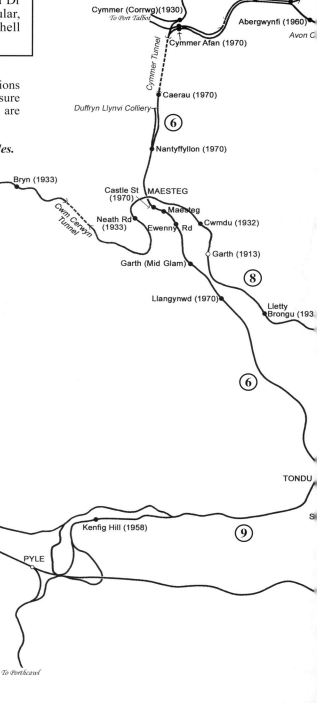

GEOGRAPHICAL SETTING

Running along the northern edge of the Vale of Glamorgan is the South Wales main line and the routes marked 1 to 7 on the map are largely within the deep coal mining valleys. No. 1 is in the valley of the River Ely, which enters the Bristol Channel near Cardiff. The valley of No. 2 is drained by Ogwr Fach into the waters of Ogwr Fawr, which flows through the Ogmore Vale, which contains route No. 3.

No. 4 is in the Cwm Garw, through which flows the Afon Garw into the Llynfi River. This drains the Llynfi Valley along which runs No. 6. These rivers join the Ogmore, which continues south alongside No. 5 to Bridgend and eventually to the sea.

No. 8 ran through extensive afforestation and across the uplands between the valleys, while No. 7 climbed along the upper part of the valley of the Afon Corrwg.

The South Wales coalfield covers an area of 518 square miles and our lines are near the centre of it, in an area known now as Mid-Glamorgan.

The maps are to the scale of 25ins to 1 mile, with north at the top unless otherwise indicated. Welsh spelling and hyphenation has varied over the years and so we have generally used the form of the period.

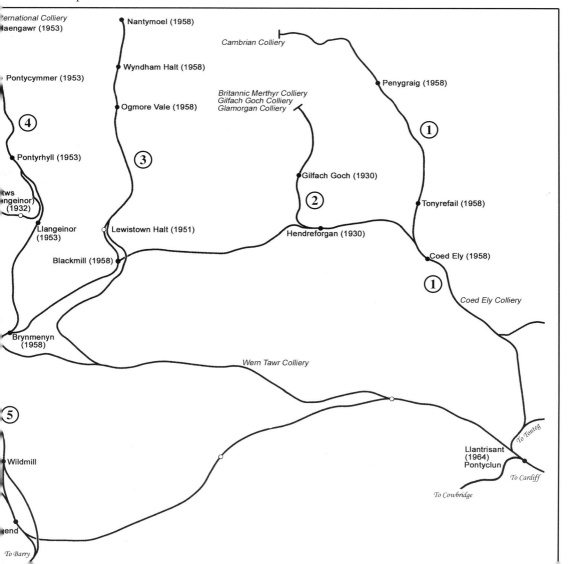

HISTORICAL BACKGROUND

South Wales Railway

This broad gauge line opened between Chepstow and Swansea in 1850 and became part of the Great Western Railway in 1863. We will simplify the developments by using the first name of the railway. For clarity, we have numbered the routes on map I.

The GWR main line was converted to standard gauge in this area in 1872. Route nos 1, 2, 5, 6 and 7 were also narrowed at the same time, but were mostly mixed gauge for a few years. The others were standard gauge from the outset.

Ely Valley Railway

This is route No. 1 and it opened north from Llantrisant to Tonyrefail in 1860 and on to Penygraig in 1862. The extension to the Clydach Vale Collieries was completed by the Ely & Clydach Vale Railway in 1878 and this part became GWR property in 1880. The first two sections did so in 1903.

Llynvi & Ogmore Railway

This company's routes are shown as Nos 2 and 3. The eastern line opened in 1865, as did the western one; the link was in use from 1876 to 1962. The lines were owned by the Ogmore Railway until 1866. The Llynvi Valley Railway opened from Bridgend to Maesteg (Nos 5 and 6) and on to Caerau Dyffryn in 1861. This also became part of the Ll&OR in 1866. The extension to Cymmer and Abergwynfi was completed in 1878 and the GWR took over in 1883.

South Wales Mineral Railway

This started in the Briton Ferry area and ran east to Cymmer. The section north to Glyncorrwg was completed in 1863 and is shown as No. 7. The SWMR became part of the GWR in 1922.

Garw Valley Branch

This was GWR owned from its opening in 1876 and is No. 4 on the map. It was always standard gauge.

Port Talbot Railway & Dock Company

Shown as No. 8, this late line came into use in 1897 and provided direct access to the ships for coal export from three productive valleys. The company also built a link between Port Talbot and the Ll&OR's 1861 line west from Tondu to Pyle, in 1898 (No. 9). The GWR took over operation of the routes in 1908.

Passenger dates are in the next section and goods closures are given in the captions. The GWR became the Western Region of British Railways upon nationalisation in 1948.

Noteworthy was the reintroduction of passenger service between Bridgend and Maesteg in 1992, prior to privatisation in 1994.

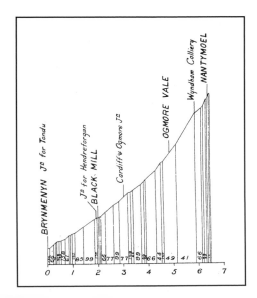

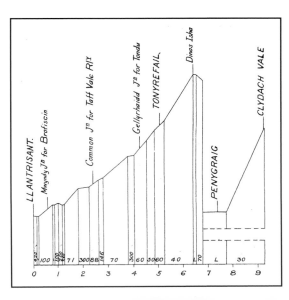

PASSENGER SERVICES

As in other Welsh valleys, the term "down" means downhill or southwards, whereas on most lines in Britain it indicates "away from London". Our examples below refer to the former in this volume. The services were mostly weekdays only. Odd days are not included. The number of trains are shown after the years.

No. 1 Ely Valley
Llantrisant to Penygraig: 1902-5, 1918-6, 1939-9 and 1957-5. Trains ran from 1st May 1901 to 9th June 1958.

No. 2 Gilfach Goch Branch
Services to Blackmill: 1882-2, 1898-3, 1915-6 and 1929-4. These reversed at Hendreforgan and were operated by the GWR from 1st September 1881 until 22nd September 1930. (Hendreforgan had a service from 1st September 1875).

No. 3 Ogmore Vale
Trains from Nantymoel generally ran to Bridgend thus: 1873-3, 1898-5, 1929-5 and 1958-6. The service ran from 12th May 1873 through to 5th May 1958.

No. 4 Garw Valley
From Blaengarw: 1902-5, 1915-6, 1929-4 and 1952-4. Trains ran to Bridgend in the early years and to Port Talbot via Maesteg (Route 8) from 1898, reverting to Bridgend in 1932.

No. 5 Tondu and
No. 6 Abergwynfi
An improving service was provided south of Maesteg, but when the route was completed northwards, only three trains used the northern terminus. Later figures were: 1918-6, 1939-8 and finally 1960-8. From 13th June 1960, the service was cut back to Cymmer Afan. It ceased totally on 22nd June 1970, but continued for scholars to 14th July 1970. It reopened between Maesteg and Bridgend with an hourly service from 28th October 1992.

No. 7 Glyncorrwg
Trains ran between Cymmer and Glyncorrwg from March 1918 until 22nd September 1930. Sample figures were July 1919-5 and July 1929 showed 2 on Fridays and 3 on Saturdays.

No. 8 East and West of Maesteg
The PTR&D carried passengers between Port Talbot Central and Pontycwmmer from 14th February 1898 until 12th September 1932. Traffic continued between the former and Maesteg Neath Road until 11th September 1933. Frequency examples were: 1899-5, 1916-5 and 1931-6. The latter figure applied west of Maesteg; there were only a few trains east thereof, Fridays and Saturdays only. Most trains ran through to Blaengarw in the later years.

No. 9 West of Tondu
Services operating between Tondu and Porthcawl ran from 10th August 1861 until 5th May 1958. Examples are 1872-3, 1899-5, 1921-6 and 1955-5.

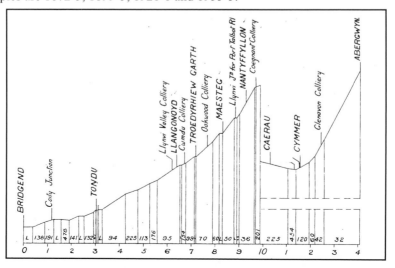

1. Ely Valley
LLANTRISANT

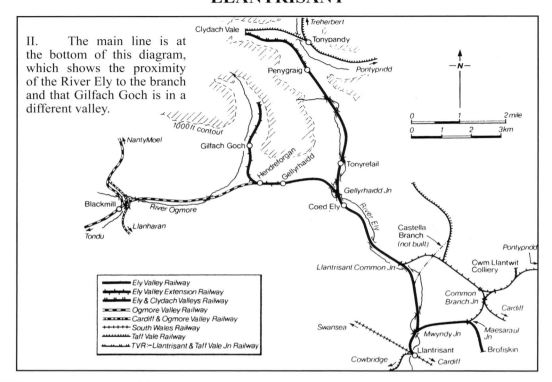

II.   The main line is at the bottom of this diagram, which shows the proximity of the River Ely to the branch and that Gilfach Goch is in a different valley.

Clydach Vale
Treherbert
Tonypandy
Penygraig
Pontypridd
1000 ft contour
NantyMoel
Gilfach Goch
Hendreforgan
Gellyrhaidd
Tonyrefail
Gellyrhaidd Jn
Blackmill
River Ogmore
Coed Ely
River Ely
Castella Branch (not built)
Pontypridd
Llanharan
Tondu
Cwm Llantwit Colliery
Llantrisant Common Jn
Common Branch Jn
Cardiff
Swansea
Mwyndy Jn
Maesaraul Jn
Brofiskin
Cowbridge
Llantrisant
Cardiff

—N—

0   1   2 mile
0   1   2   3km

——— Ely Valley Railway
⊢⊢⊢ Ely Valley Extension Railway
⊤⊤⊤ Ely & Clydach Valleys Railway
–··–··– Ogmore Valley Railway
▭▭▭ Cardiff & Ogmore Valley Railway
+++++ South Wales Railway
⋀⋀⋀ Taff Vale Railway
⊤⊤⊤ TVR:–Llantrisant & Taff Vale Jn Railway

BRIDGEND, MAESTEG, and ABERGWYNFI.—Great Western.

Down.	3 cl. (Mons. only.)	mrn	mrn (Except Saturdays)	non (Sats. only.)	aft (Sats. only.)	aft	aft	aft	aft (Sats. only.)
Bridgend ....dep.		8 47	11 9	12 0	1 27	2 22	4 52	7 39	9 37
Tondu (below)........		9 0	1122	1213	1 37	2 35	5 5	7 52	9 50
Llangonoyd		9 8	1130	1221		2 43	5 13	8 0	9 58
Troedyrhiew Garth ..		9 12	1134	1225		2 47	5 17	8 4	10 2
Maesteg	6 25	9 19	1140	1231		2 53	5 23	8 10	10 5
Tywith	6 29	9 24	1144	1235		2 57	5 27	8 14	
Cymmer * 72	6 38	9 32	1153	1244		3 6	5 36	8 23	
Abergwynfi......arr.	6 44	9 38	1159	1250		3 12	5 42	8 29	

Up.	mrn	mrn	aft (Sats. only.)	aft	aft	aft	aft
Abergwynfi ......dep.	7b5	9 57		1 10	3 58	5 58	8 40
Cymmer * 72	7b11	10 3		1 16	4 4	6 4	8 46
Tywith	7 17	10 9		1 22	4 10	6 10	8 52
Maesteg	7 22	1014		1 27	4 15	6 15	8 55
Troedyrhiew Garth ..	7 26	1018		1 31	4 19	6 19	9c1
Llangonoyd	7 30	1022		1 35	4 23	6 23	9c5
Tondu (below) ....[69	7 37	1029	1 10	1 42	4 30	6 30	9c12
Bridgend 60 to 64 arr.	7 48	1040	1 18	1 53	4 41	6 41	9c28

b Mondays only. c Saturdays only. * Station for Glyncorrwg.

BRIDGEND, PONTYCYMMER, GILFACH, and NANTYMOEL.—Great Western.

Fares. 1 cl.	2 cl.	gov	Down.	mrn	mrn (Except Saturdays.)	aft (Saturdays only.)	aft	aft	aft	aft (Saturdays only.)
			Bridgend......dep.	8 57	1116	12 7	2 29	4 59	7 46	9 44
0 6	0 4	0 3	Tondu	9 10	1129	1220	2 42	5 12	7 59	9 57
0 8	0 5	0 4	Brynmenyn ..arr.	9 13	1132	1223	2 45	5 15	8 2	10 0
....	....	....	Brynmenyn dep.	9 19	1138	1229	2 51	5 21	8 8	10 6
1 0	0 8	0 6	Llangeinor	9 26	1145	1236	2 58	5 28	8 15	1013
1 3	0 10	0 7½	Pontyrhyll	9 31	1150	1241	3 3	5 33	8 20	1018
1 5	0 11	0 8½	Pontycymmer ar	9 35	1154	1245	3 7	5 37	8 24	1022
....	....	....	Brynmenyn ..dep.	9 16	1135	1226	2 48	5 18	8 5	10 3
1 0	0 8	0 6	Blackmill	9 20	1139	1230	2 52	5 22	8 9	10 7
....	....	....	Blackmill ..dep.	9 23	....	....	2 55	5 25	8 12	....
1 6	1 0	0 9	Hendreforgan....	9 34	....	....	3 6	5 36	8 23	....
1 9	1 2	0 10½	Gilfach ......arr.	9 38	....	....	3 10	5 40	8 27	....
1 5	0 11	0 8½	Tynewydd *	9 33	1152	1243	3 5	5 35	8 22	1020
1 8	1 1	0 10	Nantymoel....arr.	9 39	1158	1249	3 11	5 41	8 28	1026

Up.	mrn	mrn	aft (Thursdays only. ☞)	aft	aft	aft	aft (Saturdays only.)
Nantymoel....dep.	7 7	9 59	....	1 12	4 0	6 0	8 42
Tynewydd *	7 13	10 5	....	1 18	4 6	6 6	8 48
Gilfach......dep.	....	9 52	1 5	....	3 53	5 53	....
Hendreforgan....	....	9 59	1 9	....	4 0	6 0	....
Blackmill ..arr.	....	10 7	1 20	....	4 8	6 8	....
Blackmill	7 20	1012		1 25	4 13	6 13	8 53
Brynmenyn ..arr.	7 24	1016		1 29	4 17	6 17	8 59
Pontycymmer dp	7 0	9 56		1 9	3 57	5 57	8 39
Pontyrhyll	7 5	10 1		1 14	4 2	6 2	8 44
Llangeinor	7 9	10 5		1 18	4 6	6 6	8 48
Brynmenyn arr.	7 14	1010		1 23	4 11	6 11	8 53
Brynmenyn.. dep.	7 27	1019		1 32	4 20	6 20	9 2
Tondu, above & below	7 33	1025		1 38	4 26	6 26	9 8
Bridgend 60, 69 ar	7 41	1033		1 46	4 34	6 34	9 18

August 1898

Fares. TONDU and PORTHCAWL.—Great Western.

Single 1 cl.	Single 2 cl.	Single gov	Return 1 cl.	Return 2 cl.	Return gov	Down.	mrn	mrn	mrn	mrn	mrn	aft	aft	aft	aft	aft	aft	aft	aft	aft	aft	Sundays mrn	Sundays af
						Tondu ....dep.	7 45	....	9 5	1040	....	....	2 0	....	....	....	5 10	....	....	....	....	....	....
0 8	0 5	0 4	1 2	0 9	0 8	Kenfig Hill	7 57	....	9 17	1052	....	....	2 12	....	....	....	5 22	....	....	....	....	....	....
1 0	0 8	0 6	1 9	1 2	1 0	Pyle 62............	8 5	9 0	9 25	11 0	1120	1245	2 32	2 50	3 54	4 45	5 30	6 15	6 45	7 30	8 40	1045	3
1 7	1 0	0 9½	2 10	1 9	1 7	Porthcawl....arr.	8 15	9 10	9 35	1110	1130	1255	2 42	3 0	4 2	4 55	5 40	6 25	6 55	7 39	8 50	1055	3 1

Single 1 cl.	Single 2 cl.	Single gov	Return 1 cl.	Return 2 cl.	Return gov	Up.	mrn	mrn	mrn	mrn	mrn	aft	aft	aft	aft	aft	aft	aft	aft	aft	aft	Sundays aft	Sundays
						Porthcawl....dep.	7 35	8 20	8 30	9 50	1022	1220	1 10	2 5	4 12	4 30	5 50	6 27	7 0	7 12	8 15	7 45	...
0 7	0 5	0 3½	1 1	0 9	0 7	Pyle 60, 62.......	7 45	8 29	8 39	10 1	1032	1230	1 20	2 15	4 22	4 40	6 0	6 36	7 10	7 21	8 25	7 54	...
1 0	0 7	0 5¼	1 9	1 1	0 11	Kenfig Hill	....	8 38	....	1010	....	....	1 30	....	....	4 50	....	....	7 22	....	....	....	...
1 7	1 0	0 9½	2 10	1 9	1 7	Tondu (see above) a	....	8 48	....	1020	....	....	1 40	....	....	5 0	....	....	7 32	....	....	....	...

July 1899

PORT TALBOT, MAESTEG, and PONTYCYMMER.—Port Talbot Railway and Docks.

Fares 1 cl.	3 cl.	Up.	mrn	mrn	aft	aft	aft	aft (Sats. only.)
		Port Talbot (Cen.) dp	....	9 30	1235	....	6 35	....
....	....	Port Talbot & Aber-	6 0	....	....	4 40	....	9 10
0 9	0 4	Bryn...........[avon	6 14	9 44	1249	4 53	6 46	9 24
1 6	0 8½	Maesteg	6 23	9 54	1259	5 2	6 55	9 34
....	....	Garth..............	....	9 59	1 4	5 7	6 59	9 39
2 0	1 0	Lletty Brongu.......	6 32	10 2	1 7	5 10	7 2	9 42
2 6	1 3	Pontyrhyll (see above)	6 40	1011	1 16	5 18	7 10	9 51
2 9	1 4½	Pontycymmer ..arr.	6 45	1015	1 20	5 22	7 14	9 55

Fares 1 cl.	3 cl.	Down.	mrn	mrn	aft	aft	aft	aft (Sats. only.)
		Pontycymmer ..dep.	8 5	1030	1 35	5 28	7 20	10
....	....	Pontyrhyll	8 10	1035	1 40	5 33	7 25	10
....	....	Lletty Brongu	8 19	1044	1 49	5 42	7 33	101
....	....	Garth..............	8 22	1047	1 52	5 45	7 36	...
....	....	Maesteg............	3 28	1053	1 58	5 51	7 40	102
....	....	Bryn...........[avon	8 37	11 2	2 7	6 0	7 49	103
....	....	Port Talbot & Aber-	....	....	2 18	....	8 0	104
2 9	1 4½	Port Talbot 62,72 ar	8 48	1113	....	6 11	....	...

1. A westward panorama from July 1959 has the Cowbridge line curving left behind the signal box, which was in use until 25th April 1966. It is facing the large goods shed. Trains used the curve to the left of it to reach Coed Ely Colliery until 2nd April 1984 and Cwm Llantwit Colliery until 2nd March 1987. (H.C.Casserley)

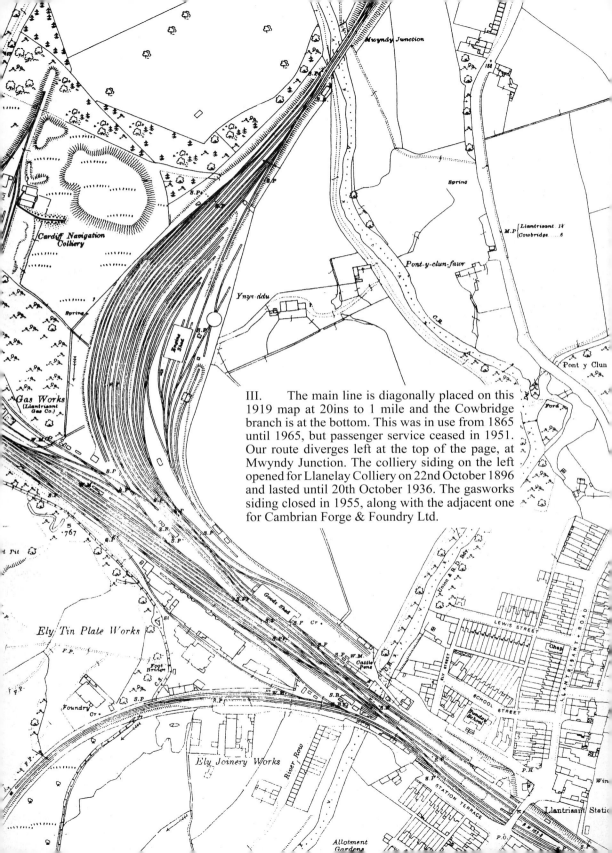

Mwyndy Junction

Spring

Llantrisant 1¼
Cowbridge 6

M.P

Pont-y-clun-fawr

Cardiff Navigation
Colliery

Ynys-ddu

Pont y Clun

Ford

Spring

Gas Works
(Llantrisant
Gas Co.)

III.   The main line is diagonally placed on this 1919 map at 20ins to 1 mile and the Cowbridge branch is at the bottom. This was in use from 1865 until 1965, but passenger service ceased in 1951. Our route diverges left at the top of the page, at Mwyndy Junction. The colliery siding on the left opened for Llanelay Colliery on 22nd October 1896 and lasted until 20th October 1936. The gasworks siding closed in 1955, along with the adjacent one for Cambrian Forge & Foundry Ltd.

Goods Shed

Pit

Ely Tin Plate Works

LEWIS STREET

Foot
Bridge

SCHOOL STREET

Foundry

Castle
Pens

River Row

Ely Joinery Works

STATION TERRACE

Llantrisant Station

Allotment
Gardens

2.   Looking in the other direction in contrasting weather on 4th January 1958, we see 0-4-2T no. 1471 ready to leave at 1.10pm for Penygraig. Cowbridge trains had earlier used the far side of the island platform on the right. The structures visible mostly date from 1899 and they were all destroyed after closure on 2nd November 1964. A new station called Pontyclun opened on the site on 28th September 1992. (H.C.Casserley)

Other photographs of the station can be seen in our *Cardiff to Swansea* album, along with views of the Cowbridge branch.

3.   The locomotive depot was photographed on 22nd September 1962, when it had the code 88G. It was in use from October 1900 to October 1964, diesels being based here subsequently. The first shed opened in 1860. (R.S.Carpenter coll.)

NORTH OF LLANTRISANT

4.	Mwyndy Junction is the location of this view of 0-6-0PT no. 4674 with a Llantrisant to Penygraig train on 13th July 1957. See our *Cardiff to Pontypridd* album for the Llantrisant-Treforest section. (S.Rickard/J&J coll.)

5.	Class 117 DMUs were used on a railtour on 31st March 1984, which included a visit to Coed Ely Colliery & Coke Ovens. The section southwards had officially closed on 4th October 1983. Northwards to Clydach Vale was lost on 2nd April 1967. The pit was sunk in 1906-09 and the works eventually became National Smokeless Fuels Ltd. Much of its output went by train to the West Midlands. (P.Jones)

COED ELY

6.   The station opened on 13th July 1925, much later than those to the north of it. No. 1471 is seen again, this time propelling a Penygraig to Llantrisant train, sometime in April 1956. Tickets issued in 1929 numbered 14,784 and in 1938 it was 7231. (R.Darlaston)

TONDU and PORTHCAWL.—Great Western.

Miles.	Down.	mrn	mrn	mrn	aft	aft	aft	aft	aft	aft	aft	aft						Sundays. mrn
	Tondu ......dep.	7 45	9 5	....	....	2 0	....	....	....	5 10	....							....
3¾	Kenfig Hill	7 57	9 17	....	....	2 14	....	....	....	5 22	....							....
6	Pyle 69...........	8	5	9 25	1125	1250	2 32	3 50	3 55	4 46	5 30	6 15	7 28					1047
9¾	**Porthcawl** ...arr.	8 15	9 35	1135	1 0	2 42	3 0	4 4	4 55	5 40	6 25	7 35						1057

Mls	Up.	mrn	mrn	mrn	mrn	aft	aft	aft	aft	aft	aft	aft	aft					aft
—	**Porthcawl** ...dep.	8 20	8 35	9 50	1020	1225	2	5	4 12	4 27	5 50	6 27	7 0					7 45
3¾	Pyle 66, 69.....	3 29	8 43	10 1	1029	1234	2 15	4 22	4 38	6 0	6 36	7 10						7 54
5¾	Kenfig Hill	8 33	....	1010	....	....	....	....	4 47	....	....	7 22						....
9¾	**Tondu** 75 ....arr.	8 43	....	1020	....	....	....	....	4 57	....	....	7 32						....

PORT TALBOT, MAESTEG, and PONTYCYMMER.—Port Talbot Railway and Docks.

Up.	mrn	mrn	aft	aft	aft		aft	Down.	mrn	mrn	aft	aft	aft		aft
Port Talbot (Cen.) dp	....	9 25	1 5	....	6 45		....	Blaengarw......dep.	8 0	1025	3 0	5 20	7 38		10 5
Port Talbot & Aber-	5 45	....	....	4 25	....		10 0	Pontycymmer........	8 5	1030	3 5	5 25	7 43		11 0
Bryn...........[avon	6 2	9 39	1 19	4 33	6 58		1014	Pontyrhyll	8 10	1035	3 10	5 30	7 48		11 5
Maesteg 75	6 14	9 48	1 29	4 42	7 7		1024	Bettws (Llangeinor).	8 14	1039	2 14	5 34	7 52		....
Garth	3 20	9 54	3 34	4 48	7 12		1632	Lletty Brongu	8 19	1044	2 19	5 39	7 57		....
Lletty Brongu	3 24	9 57	1 37	4 51	7 15		1639	Garth	8 22	1047	3 22	5 42	8 0		111
Bettws (Llangeinor)..	8 30	10 21	42	4 57	7 20		....	**Maesteg** 75	8 28	1053	3 25	5 48	8 6		1123
Pontyrhyll 75	8 35	10 8	1 45	5 1	7 24		1041	Bryn..........[avon	8 27	11 2	2 37	5 57	8 15		1125
Pontycymmer	3 40	1019	1 53	5 7	7 28		1045	Port Talbot & Aber-	....	....	....	9 50	....	3 28	1143
Blaengarw ......arr.	6 45	1015	1 55	5 10	7 33		1050	Port Talbot 69 arr.	8 43	111	....	6 10	....		....

December 1902

TONYREFAIL

IV. The 1920 edition reveals the proximity of the chapels and the cinema to the station. It also shows the long sloping paths up to the platforms. Unusually, Station Road goes to the goods yard and not the station. The former predated the latter by over 40 years. It lasted seven years longer, closing on 7th October 1963. Near the top is the 25-lever signal box (S.B.), which was open from the doubling in 1899 until 15th January 1950.

7.   No. 1471 again and we see her with the 5.12pm Penygraig to Llantrisant on 7th June 1958. Also evident is a GWR canopy, devoid of supports. The cantilever system was used at its later stations. (S.Rickard/J&J coll.)

8.   In the same year, but in foul weather, we look south and find the parcels shed nearest to us. The shed in the distance had served as the lamp room, always distant from the main buildings. A staff of 16 was listed for most of the 1930s, but this would include shunters and signalmen nearby, also Coed Ely men. (H.C.Casserley)

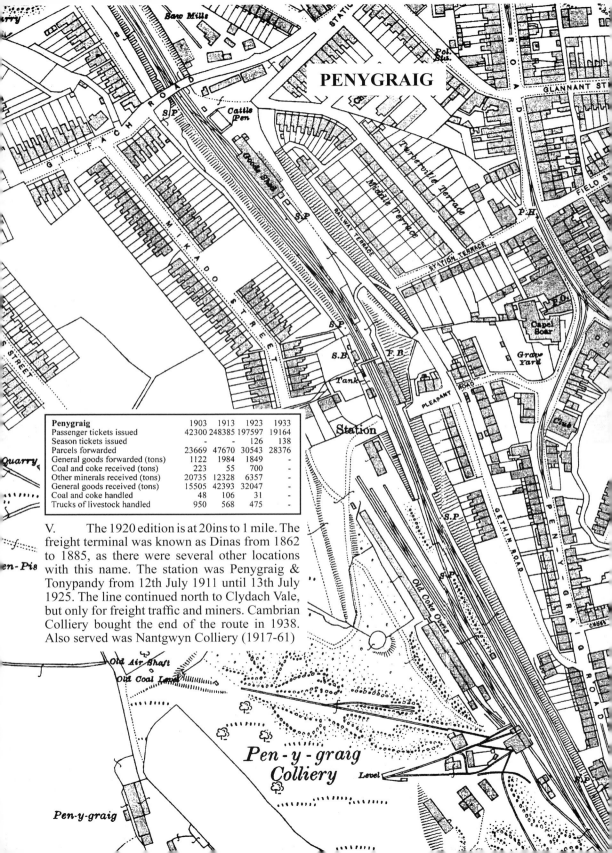

PENYGRAIG

Penygraig	1903	1913	1923	1933
Passenger tickets issued	42300	248385	197597	19164
Season tickets issued	-	-	126	138
Parcels forwarded	23669	47670	30543	28376
General goods forwarded (tons)	1122	1984	1849	-
Coal and coke received (tons)	223	55	700	-
Other minerals received (tons)	20735	12328	6357	-
General goods received (tons)	15505	42393	32047	-
Coal and coke handled	48	106	31	-
Trucks of livestock handled	950	568	475	-

V.   The 1920 edition is at 20ins to 1 mile. The freight terminal was known as Dinas from 1862 to 1885, as there were several other locations with this name. The station was Penygraig & Tonypandy from 12th July 1911 until 13th July 1925. The line continued north to Clydach Vale, but only for freight traffic and miners. Cambrian Colliery bought the end of the route in 1938. Also served was Nantgwyn Colliery (1917-61)

9.　　This panorama northwards is from the bottom edge of the map and includes the platforms, before the footbridge was erected. The bridge on the left was an aqueduct. Behind the camera was Ely Colliery (1889-1931), which was owned by the Naval Colliery Co. Ltd. It took over the one seen in 1920, the pit lasting from 1909 to 1931. Further south was Ely Rhondda Colliery (1876-1912), Cilely Colliery (1873-1953) and Collena Colliery (1891-1936). One can gasp at the chimney size. (Lens of Sutton coll.)

BRIDGEND, MAESTEG, and ABERGWYNFI.—Great Western.

Mls	Down.	3 cl.	mrn	mrn	aft	aft	aft	aft		aft	Up.	mrn	mrn	aft	aft	aft	aft	aft	aft
—	**Bridgend** ....dep.	Mons. only.	8 48	1110	1 20	2 28	4 53	7 40		9 37	**Abergwynfi** ......dep.	7 50	9 56	1 9	3 56	5 56		8 45
3	Tondu (below)........		8 59	1121	1 26	2 39	5 4	7 51		9 49	Cymmer * 76	7 58	10 2	1 15	4 2 6 2			8 51
6¼	Llangonoyd		9 7	1129		2 47	5 12	7 59		9 57	Caerau	7 513	10 7	1 20	4 7 6 7			8 56
7	Troedyrhiew Garth ..		9 12	1134		2 52	5 17	8 4		10 2	Tywith	7 18	1012	1 25	4 12 6 12			9 1
8¼	**Maesteg 76**	6 25	9 18	1140		2 58	5 23	8 10		10 8	**Maesteg 76**	7 23	1017	1 30	4 17 6 17			9 4
9¼	Tywith	6 30	9 23	1145		3 3	5 28	8 15		1013	Troedyrhiew Garth ..	7 28	1022	1 35	4 22 6 22			9c11
—	Caerau	6 34	9 27	1149		3 7	5 32	8 19		1017	Llangonoyd	7 32	1026	1 39	4 26 6 26			9c15
11½	Cymmer * 76	6 38	9 31	1153		3 11	5 36	8 23		1021	Tondu (below) ....[75	7 38	1032	1 01	4 54 4 32 6 32	7 0		9c21
14	**Abergwynfi** ......arr.	6 47	9 40	12 2		3 20	5 45	8 32		1030	**Bridgend** 66 to 71 arr.	7 47	1041	1 6	1 54 4 41 6 41	7 6		9c30

b Mondays only.　　c Saturdays only.　　* Station for Glyncorrwg.

BRIDGEND, PONTYCYMMER, GILFACH, and NANTYMOEL.—Great Western.

Mls	Down.	mrn	mrn	aft	aft	aft		aft		Mls	Up.	mrn	mrn	aft	aft	aft	aft		aft
—	**Bridgend**......dep.	8 52	1118	2 36	5 0	7 48		9 45		—	**Nantymoel** ...dep.	7 47	10 0	1 24	0 6 0		8 48		
3	Tondu	9 9	1129	2 47	5 11	7 59		9 57		1½	Ogmore Vale......	7 52	10 6	1 18	4 6 6	7	8 54		
3½	Brynmenyn ....arr.	9 12	1132	2 50	5 14	8 2		10 0		—	**Gilfach**.......dep.	7 40	9 53	1 5	3 53 5 54				
—	Brynmenyn ..dep.	9 18	1138	2 56	5 20	8	8	10 6		—	Hendreforgan	7 47	10 0	1 12	4 5 0 6 1				
5½	Llangeinor	9 25	1145	3 5	5 27	8 15		1013		—	Blackmill ...arr.	7 55	10 8	1 20	4 5 8 6 9				
7	Pontyrhyll	9 30	1150	3 8	5 32	8 20		1018		4½	Blackmill ...dep.	8 1	1014	1 26	4 14 6 15	9 2			
8¼	Pontycymmer ..arr.	9 34	1154	3 12	5 36	8 24		1022		6½	Brynmenyn ..arr.	8 5	1018	1 30	4 18 6 19	9 6			
—	**Blaengarw**	9 39	1159	3 17	5 41	8 29		1028		—	Blaengarw........	7 39	9 52	1 4 3	5 2 5 53	8 41			
—	Brynmenyn ..dep.	9 15	1135	2 53	5 17	8 5		10 3		—	Pontycymmer	7 44	9 57	1 9	3 57 5 58	8 47			
5½	Blackmill	9 19	1139	2 57	5 21	8 9		10 7		—	Pontyrhyll	7 49	10 2	1 14	4 2	8 52			
9½	Blackmill ..dep.	9 23	1142	3 0	5 25	8 15		....		—	Llangeinor	7 53	10 6	1 18	4 6 6	8 56			
—	Hendreforgan	9 34	1153	3 11	5 36	8 26		....		—	Brynmenyn ..arr.	7 58	1011	1 23	4 11 6	9 1			
11½	**Gilfach** ....arr.	9 38	1157	3 15	5 40	8 35		....		—	**Brynmenyn**......dep.	8 8	1021	1 33	21	22	9 8		
8½	Ogmore Vale......	9 29	1149	3 7	5 31	8 19		1017		7	Tondu 76 & above	8 14	1027	1 39	27	28	9 13		
10½	**Nantymoel** ..... arr.	9 38	1158	3 16	5 40	8 28		1026		10½	**Bridgend** 66, 77 arr	8 30	1041	1 45	33	34	9 19		

December 1902

10.   A northward view in 1958 includes the stream-fed water tank and the large goods shed. Freight traffic ceased on 12th October 1964, but the route was in use until 2nd April 1967. In 1923, 43 men were listed here, but it was down to 10 by 1936. (Stations UK)

11.   No. 1471 is seen working in the rain again on 4th January 1958, at the rear of the 1.10pm from Llantrisant. The signal box had 33 levers and was in use from 1st June 1911 until 9th September 1963, when the route south was singled. It had been doubled when passenger services started in 1901. (H.C.Casserley)

2. Gilfach Goch Branch
HENDREFORGAN

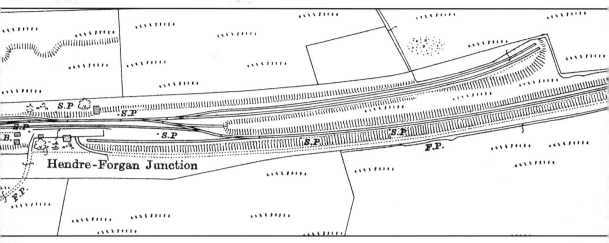

VI.　　Requests for a station to serve Gilfach eventually resulted in this remote location receiving a minimal service on 1st September 1875, but from the west at Blackmill. With great reluctance, it was extended to Gilfach on 9th May 1881, but every train had to reverse here. Withdrawal on 5th March 1928 resulted in a local rebellion, such that it was restored, but from the east, which was of little use for established business connections. Final withdrawal was on 22nd September 1930.

12.　　Although an isolated part of the Ogmore Valley Railway, the line was worked by the GWR from the outset. This view east is from April 1958 and has the site of the two long sidings in the left background. This was a desolate area of treeless bog. There was a staff of seven in 1929-30. (M.Hale)

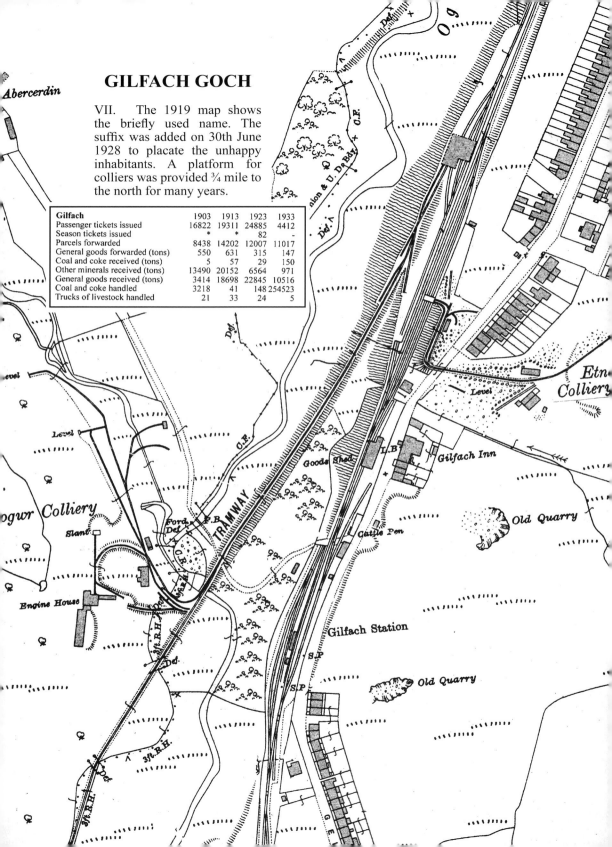

GILFACH GOCH

VII. The 1919 map shows the briefly used name. The suffix was added on 30th June 1928 to placate the unhappy inhabitants. A platform for colliers was provided ¾ mile to the north for many years.

Gilfach	1903	1913	1923	1933
Passenger tickets issued	16822	19311	24885	4412
Season tickets issued	*	*	82	-
Parcels forwarded	8438	14202	12007	11017
General goods forwarded (tons)	550	631	315	147
Coal and coke received (tons)	5	57	29	150
Other minerals received (tons)	13490	20152	6564	971
General goods received (tons)	3414	18698	22845	10516
Coal and coke handled	3218	41	148	254523
Trucks of livestock handled	21	33	24	5

Abercerdin

Etn
Colliery

Gilfach Inn

Old Quarry

Goods Shed

L.B

Cattle Pen

Old Quarry

TRAMWAY

ogwr Colliery

Slant

Ford
Def.

F.B.

Engine House

Gilfach Station

S.P

S.P

Level

Level

Def.

13.   The platform line and the run-round loop were at a lower level, as can be seen in this view south from about 1900. The signal on the left is for trains from the collieries, which included Etna (1876-1929), Glynogwr (1909-55), Glamorgan Coal (1899-1933) and Britannic Merthyr (1913-62). There were 12 employees here in 1931-38. (Lens of Sutton coll.)

14.   The remains were recorded from a railtour in 1957. A service to Tremains (west of Bridgend) had been provided for munition workers from March 1941 until June 1947. Goods traffic continued here until 5th June 1961, when the route closed. The connection to Blackmill had been lost in 1957, having been used for wagon storage for many years. It had served Glyn Ogwr Colliery (1876-1935) and Caradog Vale Colliery (1877-1935). (Stations UK)

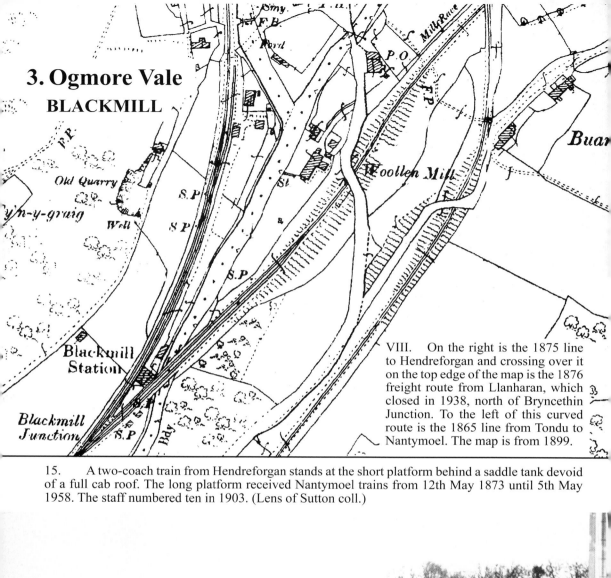

3. Ogmore Vale
BLACKMILL

VIII.   On the right is the 1875 line to Hendreforgan and crossing over it on the top edge of the map is the 1876 freight route from Llanharan, which closed in 1938, north of Bryncethin Junction. To the left of this curved route is the 1865 line from Tondu to Nantymoel. The map is from 1899.

15.   A two-coach train from Hendreforgan stands at the short platform behind a saddle tank devoid of a full cab roof. The long platform received Nantymoel trains from 12th May 1873 until 5th May 1958. The staff numbered ten in 1903. (Lens of Sutton coll.)

Blackmill	1903	1913	1923	1933
Passenger tickets issued	17573	20698	22812	2295
Season tickets issued	*	*	46	-
Parcels forwarded	1220	885	1173	1061
General goods forwarded (tons)	24	1980	115	10
Coal and coke received (tons)	229	265	261	34
Other minerals received (tons)	662	632	350	490
General goods received (tons)	152	151	721	262
Coal and coke handled	25	77	81	103
Trucks of livestock handled	4	2	2	4

16.   Looking south in June 1962, we see the 45-lever Blackmill Junction box, which was in use until 13th January 1964. The loop had been added by 1881 as traffic grew. (B.W.L.Brooksbank)

NORTH OF BLACKMILL

17.   No. 37225 is reversing over Caedu Crossing with a train for the coal washery on 26th September 1985. The box opened in 1911 and lasted until 1987. It had 17 levers and full lifting barriers came into use on 29th May 1977. The location was 2½ miles north of the station. (D.H.Mitchell)

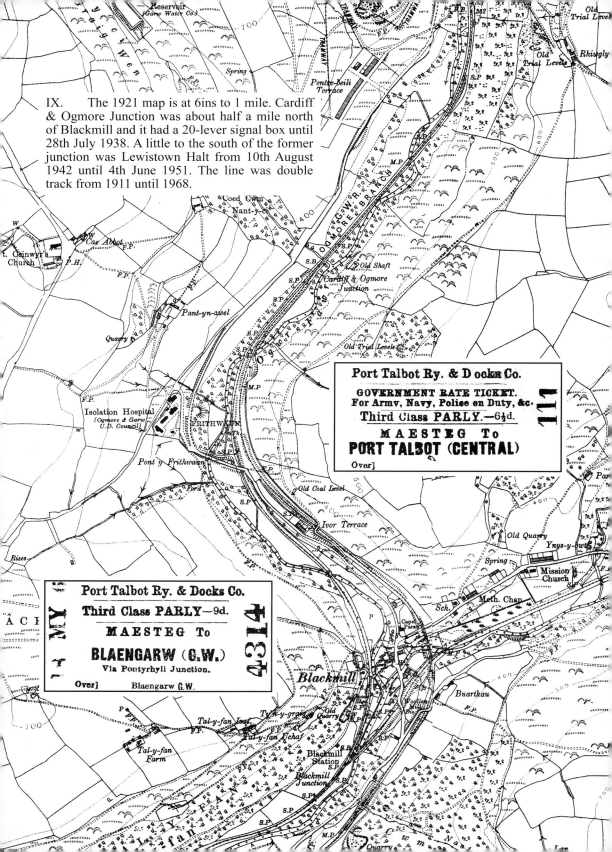

IX.   The 1921 map is at 6ins to 1 mile. Cardiff & Ogmore Junction was about half a mile north of Blackmill and it had a 20-lever signal box until 28th July 1938. A little to the south of the former junction was Lewistown Halt from 10th August 1942 until 4th June 1951. The line was double track from 1911 until 1968.

Port Talbot Ry. & Docks Co.

GOVERNMENT RATE TICKET.
For Army, Navy, Police en Duty, &c.
Third Class PARLY.—6½d.

M A E S T E G   To
PORT TALBOT (CENTRAL)

Over]

Port Talbot Ry. & Docks Co.

Third Class PARLY—9d.

M A E S T E G   To
BLAENGARW (G.W.)
Via Pontyrhyll Junction.

Over]   Blaengarw G.W.

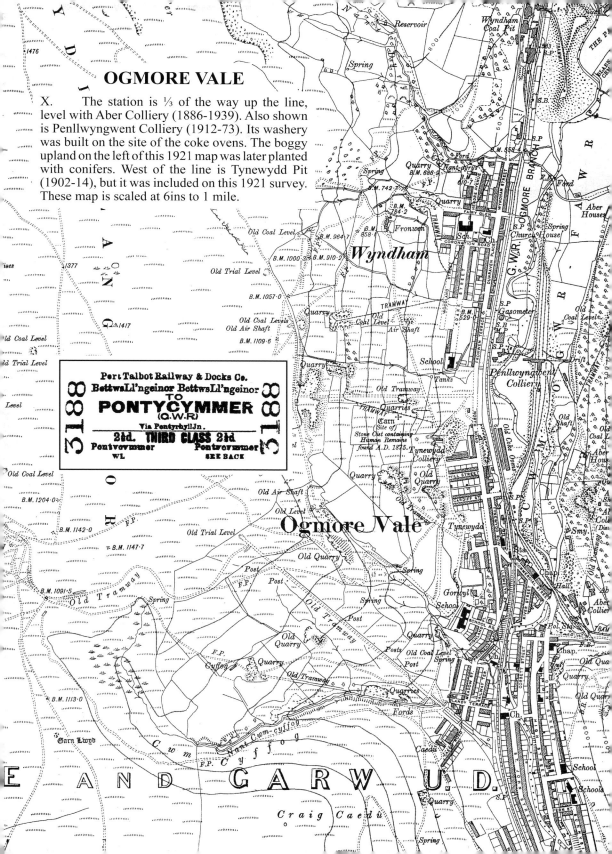

OGMORE VALE

X.   The station is ⅓ of the way up the line, level with Aber Colliery (1886-1939). Also shown is Penllwyngwent Colliery (1912-73). Its washery was built on the site of the coke ovens. The boggy upland on the left of this 1921 map was later planted with conifers. West of the line is Tynewydd Pit (1902-14), but it was included on this 1921 survey. These map is scaled at 6ins to 1 mile.

Port Talbot Railway & Docks Co.
BettwsLl'ngeinor   BettwsLl'ngeinor
TO
PONTYCYMMER
(G.W.R.)
Via Pontyrhyll Jn.
2sd.   **THIRD CLASS** 2sd.
Pontycymmer   Pontycymmer
WL   SEE BACK

3188   3188

Wyndham

Ogmore Vale

18.   No. 5524 is working an autotrain between Bridgend and Nantymoel on 3rd May 1958. South Box (left) functioned from 1892 until 17th November 1968 and had a 20-lever frame. (S.Rickard/J&J coll.)

19.   Turning round on the footbridge, we see the same train, together with North Box, which had been Middle Box until 29th October 1929. It had 45 levers. The station and boxes had been called "Tynewydd" from 22nd August 1884 until 1st January 1902. Centre is the goods yard, which closed on 23rd November 1964. There were 26 to 29 men here in 1930-38. (S.Rickard/J&J coll.)

Ogmore Vale	1903	1913	1923	1933
Passenger tickets issued	50784	78756	79330	18115
Season tickets issued	*	*	272	34
Parcels forwarded	10042	24527	26566	20475
General goods forwarded (tons)	620	1039	721	79
Coal and coke received (tons)	659	2754	377	207
Other minerals received (tons)	11797	8500	12599	2194
General goods received (tons)	4847	25912	36521	15826
Coal and coke handled	341823	486430	363906	412448
Trucks of livestock handled	29	81	86	39

20.   The decaying structure is seen some years after passenger service ceased in 1958. The gates were removed in 1974 and a flag was used thereafter. (Lens of Sutton coll.)

21.   The washery was a little to the north of the station and is seen on 23rd September 1980, as no. 37251 passes with empties for Wyndham Colliery. The wagons seem almost life expired. (D.H.Mitchell)

WYNDHAM HALT

XI.   Wyndham Pit (1878-1983) is half-way up this extract from 1921. It had a halt from 10th August 1942 to 5th May 1958, near Church House.

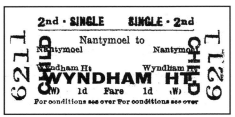

22.   The halt was on the west side of the route; the track on the left was for goods traffic. No. 5545 is bound for Nantymoel on 5th April 1958, when a return to Bridgend was on offer at 2/- and Cardiff at 2/6d. (M.Hale)

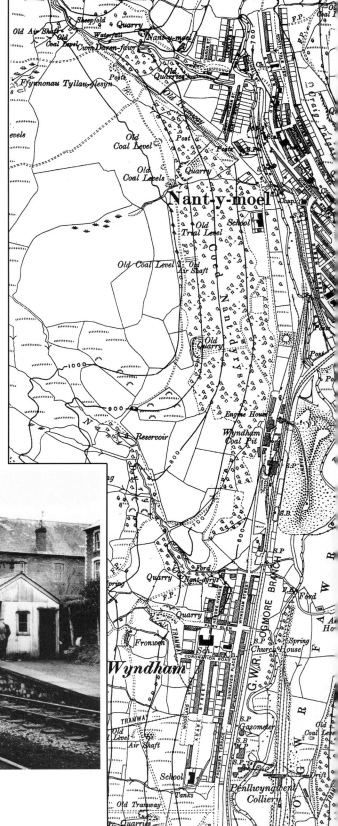

SOUTH OF NANTYMOEL

23.   No. 5524 is working to Bridgend on 3rd April 1958 and is passing Wyndham Pits South Box, which functioned from about 1925 until 24th January 1965. It had 24 levers. North Box closed in 1924. (S.Rickard/J&J coll.)

24.   A chapel is outstanding as no. 37251 is about to reverse its train into Wyndham Colliery on 23rd September 1980. Note that its brake van has been detached first. (D.H.Mitchell)

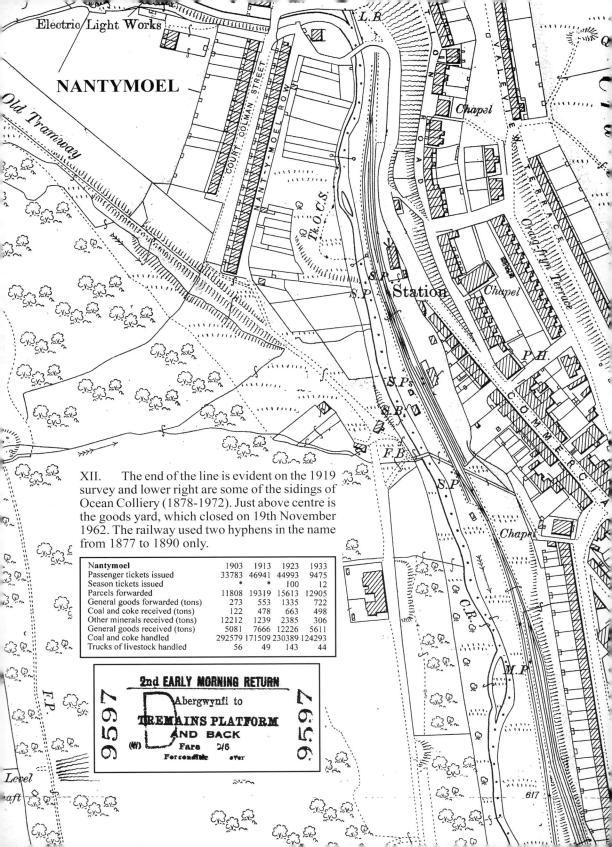

Electric Light Works

NANTYMOEL

Old Tramway

Chapel

COLMAN STREET

NANTY-MOEL-ROW

COURT

Th. O.C.S.

Chapel

L.B

VALLEY ROAD

Craig-fryn Terrace

S.P.
S.P. Station

Chapel

P.H.

S.Ps

S.B.

COMMERCIAL

F.B.

S.P.

XII.   The end of the line is evident on the 1919 survey and lower right are some of the sidings of Ocean Colliery (1878-1972). Just above centre is the goods yard, which closed on 19th November 1962. The railway used two hyphens in the name from 1877 to 1890 only.

Chapel

C.R.

M.P.

Nantymoel	1903	1913	1923	1933
Passenger tickets issued	33783	46941	44993	9475
Season tickets issued	*	*	100	12
Parcels forwarded	11808	19319	15613	12905
General goods forwarded (tons)	273	553	1335	722
Coal and coke received (tons)	122	478	663	498
Other minerals received (tons)	12212	1239	2385	306
General goods received (tons)	5081	7666	12226	5611
Coal and coke handled	292579	171509	230389	124293
Trucks of livestock handled	56	49	143	44

F.P.

9597   9597

2nd EARLY MORNING RETURN

Abergwynfi to
TREMAINS PLATFORM
AND BACK
(W)   Fare   2/6
For condition   over

Level

aft

617

25.   The end of the valley is featured in this postcard view, along with two shops. GWR livery is apparent and so it must be after 1883. (Lens of Sutton coll.)

26.   No. 4581 has arrived from Tondu on 14th July 1956 and the driver walks to his compartment at the far end of his train. There were ten employees here in 1929-30. (R.M.Casserley)

27.   No. 5524 approaches the terminus on 3rd May 1958 and single line staffs are about to be exchanged. The railings in the foreground are to prevent staff falling into a stream. (S.Rickard/J&J coll.)

28.   The drivers window and gong are featured as the same train waits to depart for Bridgend. The signal box was completed in about 1892 and it was in use until 3rd January 1964. Its 1920 frame had 31 levers. (S.Rickard/J&J coll.)

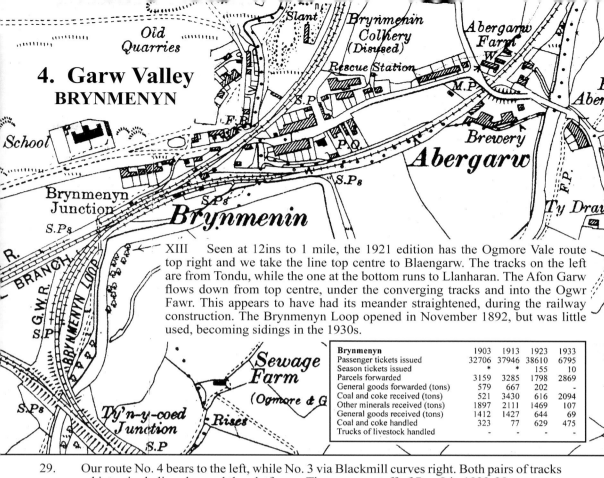

4. Garw Valley
BRYNMENYN

(map labels): Old Quarries · Slant · Brynmenin Colliery (Disused) · Abergarw Farm · Rescue Station · M.P. · Aber · School · Brewery · Abergarw · Brynmenyn Junction · Brynmenin · Ty Drau · R. OGMORE BRANCH · S.G.W.R. · BRYNMENIN LOOP · Sewage Farm (Ogmore & G · Ty'n-y-coed Junction · Rises

XIII   Seen at 12ins to 1 mile, the 1921 edition has the Ogmore Vale route top right and we take the line top centre to Blaengarw. The tracks on the left are from Tondu, while the one at the bottom runs to Llanharan. The Afon Garw flows down from top centre, under the converging tracks and into the Ogwr Fawr. This appears to have had its meander straightened, during the railway construction. The Brynmenyn Loop opened in November 1892, but was little used, becoming sidings in the 1930s.

Brynmenyn	1903	1913	1923	1933
Passenger tickets issued	32706	37946	38610	6795
Season tickets issued	*	*	155	10
Parcels forwarded	3159	3285	1798	2869
General goods forwarded (tons)	579	667	202	-
Coal and coke received (tons)	521	3430	616	2094
Other minerals received (tons)	1897	2111	1469	107
General goods received (tons)	1412	1427	644	69
Coal and coke handled	323	77	629	475
Trucks of livestock handled	-	-	-	-

29.   Our route No. 4 bears to the left, while No. 3 via Blackmill curves right. Both pairs of tracks converged into single lines beyond the platforms. There was a staff of 7 or 8 in 1923-38. (Lens of Sutton coll.)

30.   The Garw Valley platforms are featured in this view from the 1960s. The 0-6-0PT is in front of the Junction Box, which had 51 levers and closed on 23rd October 1968. (Stations UK)

31.   We are at the north end of the platform on the left of picture no. 30 on 25th March 1976. Brynmenyn Crossing Box had 14 levers and was in use here until 29th August 1973. No. 37220 is hauling coal from Garw Colliery. (T.Heavyside)

LLANGEINOR

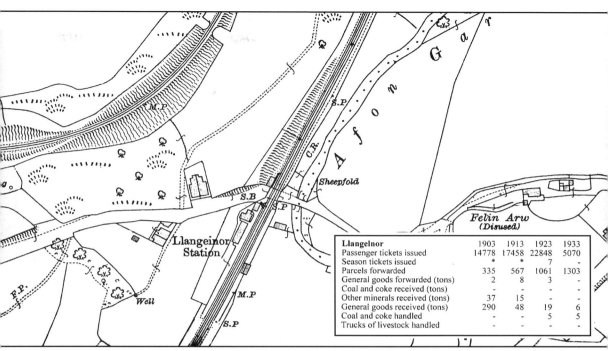

Llangeinor	1903	1913	1923	1933
Passenger tickets issued	14778	17458	22848	5070
Season tickets issued	*	*	7	-
Parcels forwarded	335	567	1061	1303
General goods forwarded (tons)	2	8	3	-
Coal and coke received (tons)	-	-	-	-
Other minerals received (tons)	37	15	-	-
General goods received (tons)	290	48	19	6
Coal and coke handled	-	-	5	5
Trucks of livestock handled	-	-	-	-

XIV.   The 1919 edition shows the river in close proximity to our route. Top left is the single line of the PTR&D. Staff numbered 5 in 1903, 3 in 1930 and thereafter they came from Pontyrhyll.

32.   A comprehensive panorama was on offer on an Edwardian postcard. This part of the route was double from 19th September 1904 to 26th October 1964. The signal box had 19 levers from 1907 and was closed on 4th December 1967, but traffic continued on the branch until 1997. (Lens of Sutton coll.)

33.　　We look south and out of view was Brynmenyn Colliery, which opened in 1901. Its loop lasted until 1965. The photograph is from 1st April 1956 and shows signals for a scissors crossover, beyond which the left track was termed an up and down goods loop. It was in use until 1959. A line to Bettws Llantwit Colliery (1880-1904) branched from it. Llangeinor Colliery (1908-11) also had a siding, plus a signal box, further north from the station. (Lens of Sutton coll.)

34.　　This view up the valley is from 13th July 1959, the route north of Brynmenyn having closed to passengers on 9th February 1953. It was also closed from 1st January 1917 to 1st January 1919, as a wartime economy measure. The gates were replaced by automatic half barriers in May 1981. (R.M.Casserley)

PONTYRHYLL

XV.   At the bottom of this 1918 edition are (from left to right) three sidings and the running line of the PTR&D, followed by one siding and two running lines of the GWR. The passenger trains of the former terminated here in their early years. The latter's line south had been doubled in 1904 and remained so until 1964. It had been doubled northwards in 1886. Near the top is Lluest Colliery (1915-32) and top left is the connection to Garw Fechan Colliery (1886-1927). Further north and on the west side was Braich y Cwmmer Colliery (also 1886-1927). Near Station Row is the signal box, which had 43 levers and was in use until 17th September 1961.

Lluest Colliery

Engine House

Reservoir

Smy.

G A R W

Lluest Colliery No.1

Old Shaft

G.W.R. GARW BRANCH

F.P.

Well

Old Quarry

Pontyrhyl

Old Quarry

Ford

Station

Meth. Chapel

Infant School

STATION ROW

Sweetwells Cottages

35.   The private siding on the right served Lluest Colliery until 1932. The bridge girders to carry the line over the river can be seen just beyond the platform. Staffing dropped from 12 in 1903 to 6 in 1935. (Lens of Sutton coll.)

Pontyrhyll	1903	1913	1923	1933
Passenger tickets issued	41254	37135	46193	10419
Season tickets issued	*	*	88	-
Parcels forwarded	1083	1157	1668	1446
General goods forwarded (tons)	581	964	458	52
Coal and coke received (tons)	1299	188	156	864
Other minerals received (tons)	8511	5334	1410	310
General goods received (tons)	8630	16699	15026	6756
Coal and coke handled	149657	238822	224710	105645
Trucks of livestock handled	45	95	151	47

36.   The staggered platforms remained to be photographed in June 1962, nine years after the last passengers had used them. On the left are the points to the goods siding, which was in use until 9th May 1960. (M.Hale)

37.   No. 37220 is working south on 25th March 1976 with coal from Garw Colliery at Blaengarw. The snow covered location is Pant-y-Gog. (T.Heavyside)

PONTYCYMMER

Ffaldau Pit

Mount Pleasant

Station

Cattle Pens

Goods Station

XVI.   The 1919 edition has Ffaldau (Victoria)
Colliery (1877-1972) on the left. The line from
the south was double from 1886 to 1964.

Pontycymmer	1903	1913	1923	1933
Passenger tickets issued	117232	123501	111737	12100
Season tickets issued	*	*	208	-
Parcels forwarded	16778	28588	25830	19601
General goods forwarded (tons)	581	964	458	52
Coal and coke received (tons)	1299	188	156	864
Other minerals received (tons)	8511	5334	1410	310
General goods received (tons)	8630	16699	15026	6756
Coal and coke handled	149657	238822	224710	95817
Trucks of livestock handled	45	95	151	47

38.   This view south from the road bridge on 13th July 1959 includes the small goods yard and large shed. They closed on 19th July 1965. The coal trains are on the lines from Ffaldau Colliery. (R.M.Casserley)

39.   We look in the other direction on the same day and see the same platform, with the other platform beyond the overbridge. Both had been out of use for six years. The 39-lever signal box was open from 1902 until 26th October 1964. There were 14 men here in 1930, dropping to 10 by 1933. (R.M.Casserley)

40. Working from Garw Colliery to Margam on the same day is 2-8-0T no. 4241. It is taking water supplied from the tank on the left. It will have passed a signal box called Victoria, which had a 31-lever frame in use until 3rd May 1964.
(R.M.Casserley)

41. No. 37225 is taking empties up to Garw Colliery on 26th September 1985. After a period of disuse, the line reopened in 1993 for the conveyance of spoil from the tips. Aberthaw Power Station was designed to use such dust and also Welsh river dredgings.
(D.H.Mitchell)

42. The route closed on 6th March 1997 and the Garw Valley Railway made plans to reopen the line from here to Bryngarw Country Park, north of Brynmenyn. The Vale of Glamorgan Railway moved much of its stock from Barry Island and a depot building was constructed by the Bridgend Valleys Railway Company Ltd., which was formed in 2001. The depot was photographed on 17th March 2007, along with *Pamela*, a 1956 Hunslet 0-6-0ST which had worked in the local collieries. (BVRC)

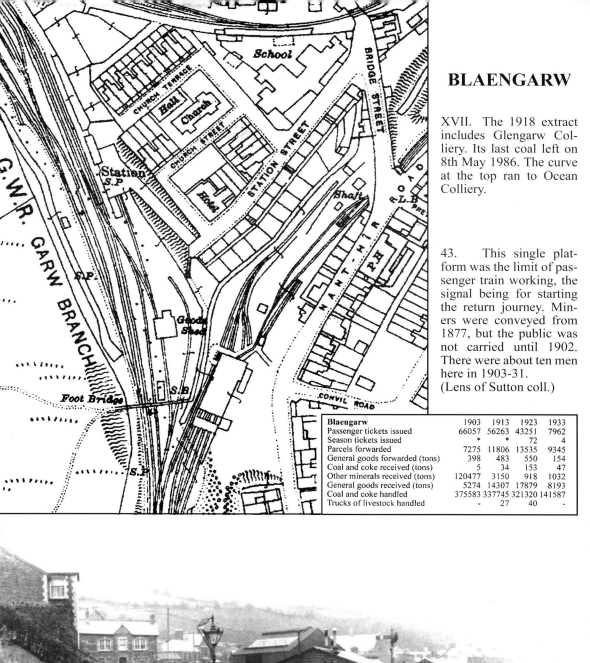

BLAENGARW

XVII. The 1918 extract includes Glengarw Colliery. Its last coal left on 8th May 1986. The curve at the top ran to Ocean Colliery.

43. This single platform was the limit of passenger train working, the signal being for starting the return journey. Miners were conveyed from 1877, but the public was not carried until 1902. There were about ten men here in 1903-31.
(Lens of Sutton coll.)

Blaengarw	1903	1913	1923	1933
Passenger tickets issued	66057	56263	43251	7962
Season tickets issued	*	*	72	4
Parcels forwarded	7275	11806	13535	9345
General goods forwarded (tons)	398	483	550	154
Coal and coke received (tons)	5	34	153	47
Other minerals received (tons)	120477	3150	918	1032
General goods received (tons)	5274	14307	17879	8193
Coal and coke handled	375583	337745	321320	141587
Trucks of livestock handled	-	27	40	-

44. Another early postcard and this shows the goods shed more clearly. Goods traffic continued until 2nd July 1962.
(Lens of Sutton coll.)

45. The posters are peeling in July 1959 as passengers had vanished six years earlier. The nearby collieries were Glengarw (1910-86) and International (1889-1967), both very productive. (R.M.Casserley)

46. The entire run-round loop was recorded during a railtour in 1960, together with the incline to the collieries. The last train of coal left here on 8th May 1986. In the distance is the 43-lever signal box, which was in use until 3rd May 1964. (Stations UK)

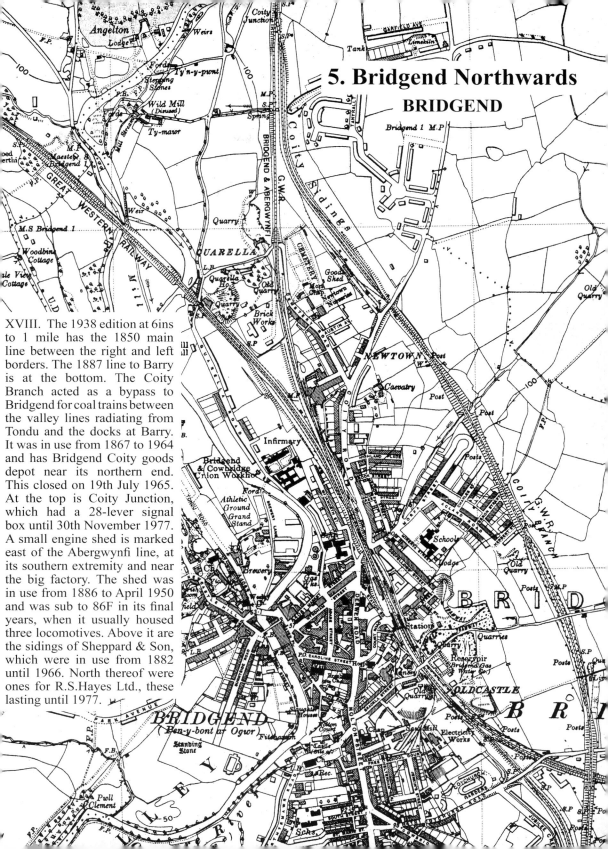

XVIII. The 1938 edition at 6ins to 1 mile has the 1850 main line between the right and left borders. The 1887 line to Barry is at the bottom. The Coity Branch acted as a bypass to Bridgend for coal trains between the valley lines radiating from Tondu and the docks at Barry. It was in use from 1867 to 1964 and has Bridgend Coity goods depot near its northern end. This closed on 19th July 1965. At the top is Coity Junction, which had a 28-lever signal box until 30th November 1977. A small engine shed is marked east of the Abergwynfi line, at its southern extremity and near the big factory. The shed was in use from 1886 to April 1950 and was sub to 86F in its final years, when it usually housed three locomotives. Above it are the sidings of Sheppard & Son, which were in use from 1882 until 1966. North thereof were ones for R.S.Hayes Ltd., these lasting until 1977.

47. This westward view includes a representation of Brunel's chalet style station building on the down side. After the LVR arrived from Tondu, it built a separate station east of the main one, as the track gauges differed. (C.G.Maggs coll.)

48. The main lines are on the right and an 0-6-0PT waits at the island platform in August 1951, with a train for Tondu. (NRM)

49. A panorama of the southern part of the station includes the remainder of the down platform. Standing at it on 4th July 1955 is 4-6-0 no. 5049 *Earl of Plymouth* with a Fishguard to Paddington parcels train. The leading vehicle carries gas cylinders for kitchen car supply. The bay platform on the left was for services to Barry. These were discontinued from 15th June 1964 until 12th July 2005, although the route remained open for freight and diversions. (S.Rickard/J&J coll.)

50.   It is 7th March 1998 and no. 158821 runs in while working a Carmarthen to Manchester service. On the right no. 143617 waits to return to Maesteg. This former through platform had become a bay and was in use that day owing to flooding on the main line. (A.C.Hartless)

Other views can be seen in our *Branch Lines around Barry* and *Cardiff to Swansea* albums.

51.   The exterior was recorded on 13th February 2009, it having been renovated extensively in 1979 to conserve the remaining features from the Brunel era. The south wing had been replaced by a new entrance building with a flat roof. It carries the name of Pen-y-Bont/Bridgend, but this did not appear on timetables and tickets. The station received a new footbridge, with lifts and ramps in 2011. (V.Mitchell)

WILDMILL

52.   New stations were provided following the reopening of the line to Maesteg to passengers on 26th October 1992. They served old and new housing developments and no. 158829 is seen on 18th May 2011. (D.K.Jones)

SARN

53.   This platform was built on the west side of the line and is seen on the same day. It is just south of the site of Aberkenfig station, which was in timetables from April 1869 to January 1870. The next station is Tondu, which appears in the final section of this album. (D.K.Jones)

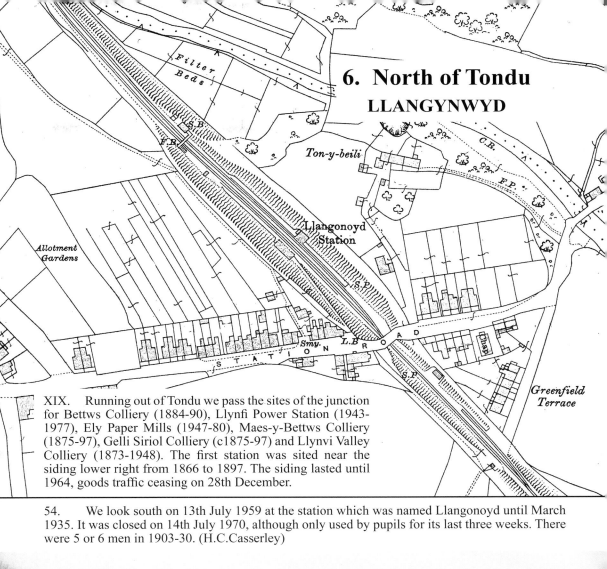

6. North of Tondu
LLANGYNWYD

Filter Beds

Ton-y-beili

Llangonoyd Station

Allotment Gardens

Greenfield Terrace

XIX.   Running out of Tondu we pass the sites of the junction for Bettws Colliery (1884-90), Llynfi Power Station (1943-1977), Ely Paper Mills (1947-80), Maes-y-Bettws Colliery (1875-97), Gelli Siriol Colliery (c1875-97) and Llynvi Valley Colliery (1873-1948). The first station was sited near the siding lower right from 1866 to 1897. The siding lasted until 1964, goods traffic ceasing on 28th December.

54.   We look south on 13th July 1959 at the station which was named Llangonoyd until March 1935. It was closed on 14th July 1970, although only used by pupils for its last three weeks. There were 5 or 6 men in 1903-30. (H.C.Casserley)

55.　　Running in from the south on 13th August 1962 is 2-6-2T no. 4121 with the 12.45pm Bridgend to Blaengwynfi service. The crossing was for use by passengers. South of the station was a siding to Garth Merthyr Colliery in about 1904-31. (L.W.Rowe)

56.　　A northward view in April 1963 shows that, while the public walked across the track, the signalman was provided with a bridge. The box had 13 levers and was in use until 17th May 1965, controlling the passing loop. (P.J.Garland/R.S.Carpenter)

GARTH (MID GLAMORGAN)

57.   The name was Troedyrhiew Garth from its opening in 1874 until its closure in 1970 (as in caption 54). No. 4121 is seen again, but on 14th July 1959 with the 1.30pm Bridgend to Cymmer Afan. North of the station were sidings for Maesteg Tinplate Works (1885-98 and 1903-38). These were also used for public goods traffic in 1947-63. Further north was Oakwood Colliery (c.1897-1930) and also Llynfi Valley Gasworks, where there was a siding from about 1885 to 1958. Four men were listed in 1929-30. (R.M.Casserley)

58.   A fresh platform was built in 1992 for the restored service, a little to the north of the original one. No. 143601 is working the 13.15 Maesteg to Coryton service on 12th December 2002, with Winter protective garments in place. (A.C.Hartless)

Troadyrhiew Garth	1903	1913	1923	1933
Passenger tickets issued	13193	7256	16148	1309
Season tickets issued	29472	48132	45037	19918
Parcels forwarded	1459	2416	3675	1970
General goods forwarded (tons)	131	178	1218	-
Coal and coke received (tons)	1596	17	48	-
Other minerals received (tons)	5506	724	863	8
General goods received (tons)	3100	2013	1695	218
Coal and coke handled	10080	17620	1498	-
Trucks of livestock handled	-	-	-	-

MAESTEG (EWENNY ROAD)

59.   We examine the two northerly stations of the 1992 group on 13th February 2009. This one was on an entirely new site on the expanded southern part of the town. (V.Mitchell)

MAESTEG

60.   The new terminus was built south of the town centre before reaching the site of the original station. Its land had been redeveloped. No. 158838 and its crew are taking a break before returning at 11.17 on the same day. (V.Mitchell)

MAESTEG
(CASTLE STREET)

XX. The 1919 edition at 20ins to 1 mile has our route from bottom to top, the line being doubled north to Llynfi Junction on 1st June 1885. The PTR&D track passes over it at the top and curves down to the right, on its way to Pontyrhyll. The cattle pens were built on the site of a small engine shed, which closed in October 1887. There was a turntable east of it and the platforms were further east until 1898, when the one marked was completed. The goods yard was developed at the same time.

61.　A view down the valley includes Castle Street signal box. It had been North Box from its opening in 1897 until 1st July 1924, when the station received that suffix. The frame had 33 levers and was taken out of use on 9th May 1971. South Box (35 levers) closed on the same day. (Lens of Sutton coll.)

Maesteg (Castle Street)	1903	1913	1923	1933
Passenger tickets issued	169756	282353	328129	115350
Season tickets issued	*	*	502	435
Parcels forwarded	7470	60701	50736	49401
General goods forwarded (tons)	1591	1864	1000	696
Coal and coke received (tons)	2529	5087	3762	2926
Other minerals received (tons)	11078	5817	5957	2400
General goods received (tons)	14835	22353	16303	9907
Coal and coke handled	99567	123362	62673	239092
Trucks of livestock handled	235	210	253	151

62.　No. 5556 runs in with the 12.50pm Abergwynfi to Bridgend train on 29th September 1951, while parcel traffic awaits. The high ground in the background needed a long tunnel to reach Cymmer. The staff numbered 30 to 36 in 1930-38. (W.A.Camwell/SLS coll.)

63. The same train was recorded moments later as a perambulator leaves the barrow crossing. Waiting near the goods shed is 0-6-0PT no. 3699. The building had been extended in 1904 and lost its track in 1969. (W.A.Camwell/ SLS coll.)

64. A Bridgend to Blaengwynfi train passes the goods yard on 23rd July 1960, where traffic ceased on 23rd March 1981. The yard had a 6-ton crane in 1938 and its final two sidings were for coal traffic only. (E.Wilmshurst)

65. Staffing ceased on 26th February 1968 and the weeds soon took over. Public service ceased on 22nd June 1970 and so this photograph may be between those dates. (SLS coll.)

NORTH OF MAESTEG

66.   No. 37258 is shunting on 15th April 1982, before taking its train to Ogmore Washery. The tip has been partially removed, probably to Aberthaw. (P.Shannon)

67.   This is just south of Llynfi Junction, where the 1885 23-lever signal box operated until 21st November 1973. It is near the rear of the train, which is hauled by no. D6927 on 24th May 1973. The National Coal Board lines are high up on the right. The North's Navigation Railway ran to the left of the box and it served Llynfi Ironworks and Maesteg Deep Colliery, plus other sites. The box is at the bottom of the next map. (T.Heavyside)

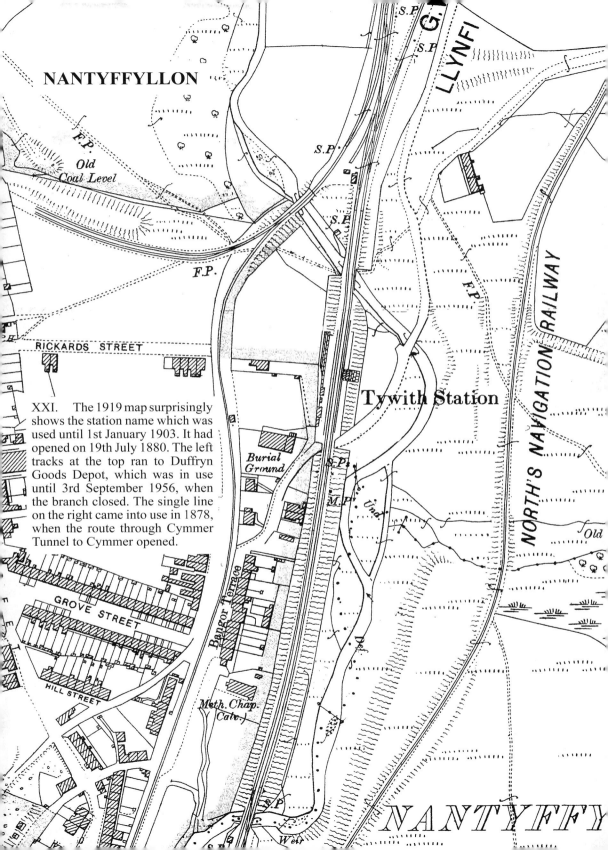

NANTYFFYLLON

F.P.

Old
Coal Level

F.P.

S.P.

S.P.

S.P.

F.P.

RICKARDS STREET

S.P.

G.

LLYNFI

NORTH'S NAVIGATION RAILWAY

F.P.

Old

Tywith Station

XXI. The 1919 map surprisingly shows the station name which was used until 1st January 1903. It had opened on 19th July 1880. The left tracks at the top ran to Duffryn Goods Depot, which was in use until 3rd September 1956, when the branch closed. The single line on the right came into use in 1878, when the route through Cymmer Tunnel to Cymmer opened.

Burial
Ground

S.P.

M.P.

Und.

GROVE STREET

Bangor Terrace

HILL STREET

Meth. Chap.
(Calv.)

S.P.

NANTYFFY

F.P.

Weir

68.   A northward view from a postcard has Northern Extension Junction in the distance. It was renamed Nantyffyllon North on 1st January 1903, when the box had 20 levers. South Box had 10 and both closed in 1966. (Lens of Sutton coll.)

69.   It is July 1959 and only one signal had been needed for three years. There were 16 men to cover here and Caerau in 1930-38. (H.C.Casserley)

70. The 12.40pm Abergwynfi to Bridgend approaches on 27th July 1960. The river bridge is in the foreground and the line north thereof was not used after 7th March 1977. (H.C.Casserley)

NORTH OF NANTYFFYLLON

71. The Llynfi River was small at this altitude of around 600ft. High in the treeless landscape on 24th May 1973 is a NCB train with coal from Coegnant Colliery destined for Maesteg Washery. The former was worked from 1882 until 1981. (T.Heavyside)

72. It is 13th June 1973 and Bagnall 0-6-0ST no. 2268 brings empties from Maesteg into Caerau Colliery. It opened in 1891 and by 1913 it employed 1998 men. In 1958, it had 732 miners and produced 173,166 tons of coal. Closure came on 26th July 1977. (D.Eatwell/M.Dart coll.)

73. We are still in the extensive workings of Caerau Colliery in May 1973 and witness Hunslet no. 3781 *Linda* leaving with coal which has been loaded in the background and will go to Maesteg for washing and grading. (T.Heavyside)

CAERAU

XXII.   The station opened on 1st April 1901 in which year the village housed 229 souls. There were many more by the time of this 1919 survey. Beyond the lower border was the 25-lever signal box, which functioned until 8th May 1971, when the line to Maesteg was singled. It was closed to Nantyffyllon on 19th July 1976.

Station

Blaen-Llynfi

Chap.

Police Station

S.P.

Library & Institute

Chap.

WESLEY STREET

LIBRARY STREET

LLOYD STREET

S.B.

Coliseum

TALANA TERRACE

GROSVENOR TERRACE

Infant School

School

School

HERMON ROAD

CARMEN STREET

GELLI STREET

Burial Ground

Chap.

Chap.

F.B.

EVANS TERRACE

BRIDGEND G.W.R. & ABERGWYNFI

S.P.

M.P.
S.P.

Ty Gwyn

P.H.

S.P.

Football Ground

Cr

Goods

Ty-gwyn-bâch Colliery

74. The GWR cantilevered canopy design avoided the provision of supports on the platform. We look north in July 1959, but the tunnel mouth is just out of view, beyond the double-armed signal post. (H.C.Casserley)

75. This 1962 record demands little comment, other than that a trip to Cardiff was on offer for five shillings. (D.K.Jones coll.)

76. The era was not recorded. It seems that a gate was the only platform facility in use towards the end, which came on 22nd June 1970, but 14th July for school pupils. A single such diesel unit left Treherbert for Bridgend once every two hours, between 1962 and 1968, on each weekday. (SLS coll.)

WEST OF CYMMER AFAN

77.   This is the northern portal of Cymmer Tunnel, which was 159yds in length. It opened for freight in July 1878 and passengers in July 1880. Featured is Cymmer South Junction, in 1959; it is lower left on the next map. (H.C.Casserley)

78.   North of the tunnel mouth is the 150yd-long Cymmer Viaduct, which is seen in a southward panorama in August 1959. An 0-6-0PT is shunting and below it is the bridge over the former Rhondda & Swansea Bay lines. Pit props are in the foreground on a siding parallel to the ex-South Wales Mineral Railway, which is at the top of the map. (S.P.Derek)

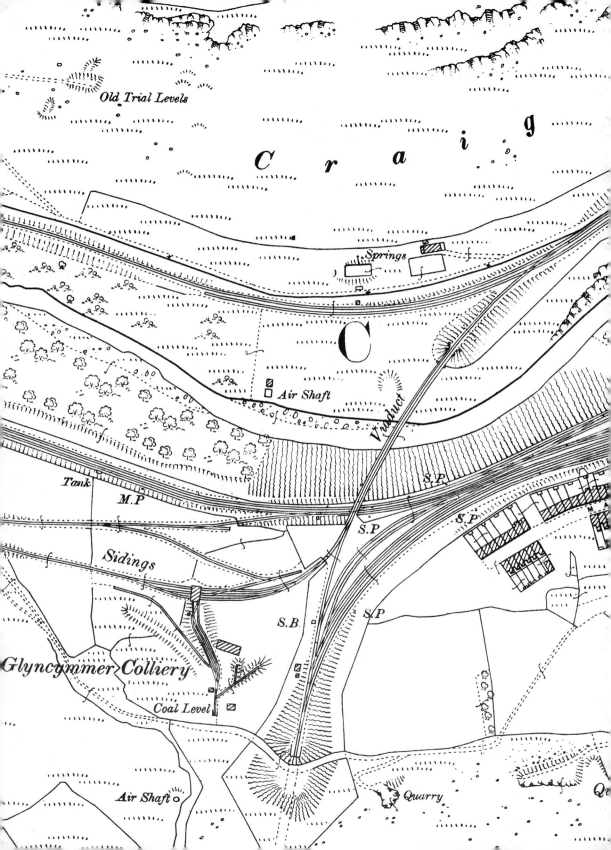

Old Trial Levels

C r a i g

Springs

C

☐ Air Shaft

Viaduct

S. P.

Tank

M.P

S. P.

Sidings

S. P.

S. B.

S. P.

Glyncymmer Colliery

Coal Level

Air Shaft o

Quarry

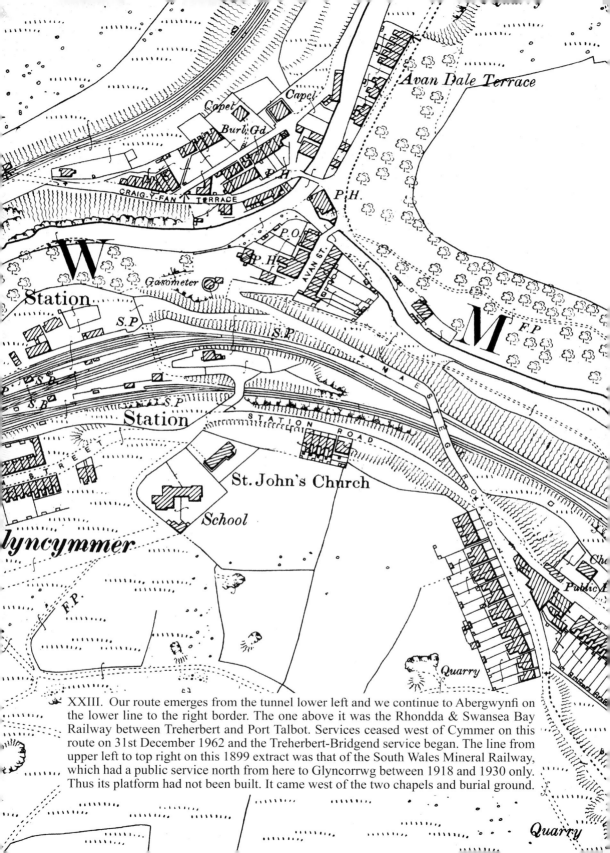

Avan Dale Terrace

Capel

Capel

Bur¹. G⁴.

P. H.

CRAIG-Y-FAN TERRACE

P. H.

P. O.

P. H.

Avan St.

W

Station

Gasometer

S. P.

S. P.

M

F. P.

S. B.

S. P.

S. B.

Station

STREET

STATION ROAD

St. John's Church

School

lyncymmer

F. P.

Quarry

Public H

Chu

XXIII. Our route emerges from the tunnel lower left and we continue to Abergwynfi on the lower line to the right border. The one above it was the Rhondda & Swansea Bay Railway between Treherbert and Port Talbot. Services ceased west of Cymmer on this route on 31st December 1962 and the Treherbert-Bridgend service began. The line from upper left to top right on this 1899 extract was that of the South Wales Mineral Railway, which had a public service north from here to Glyncorrwg between 1918 and 1930 only. Thus its platform had not been built. It came west of the two chapels and burial ground.

Quarry

79.　　The junction on the right is the one seen in picture 77 and the viaduct is on the left. We will travel on the curve on the right, the station being hidden by the large building. (P.J.Garland/R.S.Carpenter)

80.　　Another view from 1960 and we look at the other side of the 1878 viaduct from above the SWMR platform, which was known as Cymmer Corrwg. The 0-6-0PT is no. 9634. (G.Adams/M.J.Stretton coll.)

CYMMER AFAN

81.   A northward panorama from the footbridge in January 1958 has the ex-GWR station on the line to Abergwynfi in the foreground and the ex-R&SBR one in the centre. This was the only building not to be demolished. It became the village pub and was named "The Refresh", as it had contained the refreshment room. The GWR station had been known as General from 1st July 1924 until 1950, when the two stations were treated as one. (H.C.Casserley)

82.   Shunting on 13th July 1959 is 0-6-0PT no. 4640, while a sister engine waits to leave for Port Talbot. The signal box is ex-GWR. Both this and the one on the right were replaced by a new one with 51 levers - see picture 84. (H.C.Casserley)

83. The footbridge joined the platforms of the two companies, but these were altered in 1960. The R&SBR down platform gained a new face on its south side and the up one lost its track. The GWR platform is seen here receiving the 2.33pm Abergwynfi-Bridgend service, which was hauled by no. 3267 on 29th August 1959. The platform became a bay in 1960 and was little used thereafter. (S.P.Derek)

84. No. 5545 runs in with the 11.25am Bridgend to Abergwynfi on 16th April 1960 and the new signal box stands between its predecessors ready to open on 17th June. It was moved to Bargoed in 1970. (D.K.Jones)

85.   A Treherbert to Bridgend service was recorded at the new platform on 1st March 1969. There had been a bidirectional goods loop on the right of the picture, but all lines were closed on 14th December 1970. The goods yard had been on the right and this traffic ceased on 7th June 1965. It had a 2-ton crane. (M.Furnell)

**Other views can be found in pictures 97-102
in our *Pontypridd to Port Talbot* album.**

EAST OF CYMMER AFAN

86.   This is the closest that the GWR and R&SBR came, and passing the site is an 0-6-0PT taking empty stock to Abergwynfi to form the 6.30pm down train on 2nd September 1959. To avoid repairs to the nearby viaduct in 1960, the former route was connected to the latter one east of the station and an opposite link made further east. (S.P.Derek)

ABERGWYNFI

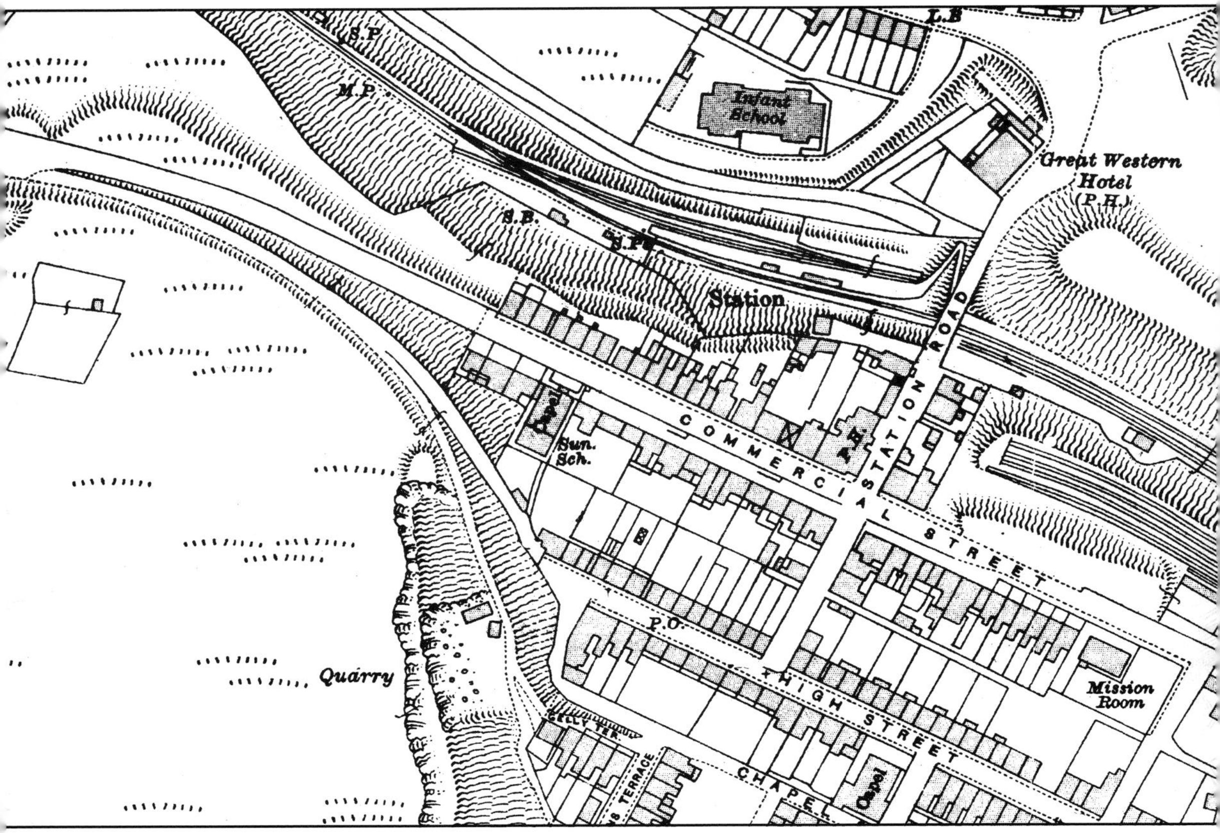

BRIDGEND, BLAENGARW, BLACKMILL, GILFACH, and NANTYMOEL.—Great Western.

Down.	Week Days only. mrn	mrn	aft	aft	aft (Saturdays only.)	aft (Saturdays only.)	aft (Saturdays only.)
Bridgend ....dep.	9 0	1132	2 20	4 52	....	7 57	1120
Tondu	9 9	1141	2 30	5 1	7 23	8 6	1128
Brynmenyn ....arr.	9 12	1144	2 33	5 4	7 26	8 9	1131
Brynmenyn ......dep.	9 18	1150	2 39	5 10	....	8 15	1140
Llangeinor	9 25	1157	2 46	5 17	....	8 22	1147
Pontyrhyll 121	9 30	12 2	2 51	5 22	....	8 27	1153
Pontycymmer	9 38	12 8	2 57	5 28	....	8 33	12 0
Blaengarw.......arr.	9 41	1211	3 0	5 31	....	8 36	12 3
Brynmenyn........dep.	9 15	1147	2 36	5 7	7 27	8 12	1133
Blackmill ....arr.	9 20	1152	2 41	5 12	7 32	8 17	1138
Blackmill ....dep.	9 27	1154	2 43	5 18	....	8 22	1143
Hendreforgan........	9 38	12 5	2 54	5 29	....	8 36	1154
Gilfach.. ....arr.	9 42	12 9	2 58	5 33	....	8 40	1158
Blackmill..........dep	9 22	1155	2 43	5 14	....	8 19	1140
Ogmore Vale	9 33	12 4	2 52	5 23	....	8 28	1151
Nantymoel.......arr.	9 39	1210	2 58	5 29	....	8 34	1157

Miles	Up.	Week Days only. mrn	mrn	aft	aft	aft	aft	aft
	Nantymoel ....dep.	7 56	10 7	1240	3 32	4 4	6 2	9 4
1½	Ogmore Vale	8 3	1014	1248	3 39	4 11	6 9	9 11
4½	Blackmill..........arr.	8 9	1021	1255	3 46	4 15	6 16	9 17
—	Mls **Gilfach**.......dep.	7 50	9 58	1233	3 23	....	5 54	8s55
—	1¼ Hendreforgan.....	7 57	10 5	1240	3 30	....	6 1	9s 3
—	4¾ Blackmill.....arr.	8 5	1013	1248	3 38	....	6 9	9s11
—	Blackmill ....dep.	8 11	1023	1256	3 47	4 17	6 17	9 18
6½	Brynmenyn ....arr.	8 15	1027	1 0	3 51		6 21	9 22
—	Mls **Blaengarw**...dep.	7 49	9 57	1232	3 22	Sats. only.	5 53	8 56
—	¾ Pontycymmer.....	7 54	10 2	1237	3 27		5 58	9 1
—	2¼ Pontyrhyll	7 59	10 7	1242	3 32		6 3	9 6
—	3½ Llangeinor........	8 3	1011	1246	3 36		6 7	9 11
—	5½ Brynmenyn ..arr.	8 8	1016	1251	3 41		6 12	9 16
—	Brynmenyn ....dep.	8 18	1030	1 3	3 54	4 22	6 24	9 23
7¼	Tondu 70 *& below*.....	8 24	1035	1 9	4 0	4 28	6 30	9a28
10¼	**Bridgend 56, 60** ...arr	8 30	1042	1 15	4 6	4 34	6 36	9a34

a 10 minutes later on Saturdays. *s* Saturdays only.

August 1915

BRIDGEND, MAESTEG, CYMMER, and ABERGWYNFI.—Great Western.

Down.	Week Days only. mrn	mrn	mrn	mrn	aft (Saturdays only.)	aft	aft (Sats. only.)	aft (Sats. only.)	aft	aft (Sats. only.)	aft (Saturdays only.)	aft (Saturdays only.)	aft	aft (Sats. only.)	aft (Sats. only.)	aft (Sats. only.)	aft (Sats. only.)	aft (Sats. only.)	aft (Saturdays only.)
Bridgend ....dep.	....	8 48	1043	1125	1 10	2 13			4 39		6 27	....	7 49						1110
Tondu	....	8 59	1050	1134	1 18	2 22			4 48		6 36	7 45	7 58						1118
Llangonoyd	....	9 8	....	1143	1 27	2 31			4 57		6 45	7 54	8 7						1127
Troedyrhiew Garth	....	9 11	....	1146	1 30	2 34			5 0		6 48	7 57	8 10						1131
Maesteg *121.............	7 40	9 20	....	1153	1 36	2 41	4 10	4 53	5 7	6 25	6 54	8 4	8 17	9 7	10 0	1015	11 0	1125	1138
Nantyffyllon	7 44	9 25	....	1158	1 40	2 46	4 15	4 58	5 12	6 30	6 59	8 9	8 22	9 12	10 5	1020	11 6	1131	1144
Caerau	7 49	9 32	....	12 5	1 47	2 53	4 20	5 4	5 19	6 35	7 4	8 15	8 29	9 18	1011	1026	1113	1138	1150
Cymmer ‡ 121	7 53	9 39	....	1212	1 50	3 0	4 23	5 7	5 26	6 38	7 7	8 18	8 36	9 23	1014	1033	1117	1142	1156
Abergwynfi ....arr.	8 0	9 45	....	1218	....	3 6	....	....	5 32	....	....	....	8 42	9 31	....	1041	....	....	12 4

Up.	Week Days only. mrn	mrn	aft (Saturdays only.)	aft	aft	aft	aft	aft (Saturdays only.)	aft	aft	aft (Saturdays only.)	aft	aft	aft	aft	aft
Abergwynfi ....dep.	8 12	10 0		1232	....	3 23	....	....	....	5 53	....	....	....	8 55	9 40	1055
Cymmer ‡ 121	8 19	10 9		1239	2 30	3 31	4 30	5 45	5 53	6 1	6 45	7 15	8 37	9 2	9 46	11 1
Caerau	8 23	1015		1245	2 35	3 37	4 35	5 50	5 58	6 7	6 50	7 20	8 42	9 7	9 51	11 6
Nantyffyllon	8 27	1020		1250	2 40	3 42	4 40	5 55	6 3	6 12	6 55	7 25	8 47	9 11	9 57	1111
Maesteg *121.............	8 31	1026		1256	2 44	3 48	4 43	6 0	6 6	6 18	7 5	7 28	8 50	9 16	10 0	1114
Troedyrhiew Garth	8 35	1030		1 1	Sats. only.	3 52	Sats. only.	....	Sats. only.	6 22	7 10	Sats. only.	Sats. only.	9 20	Sats. only.	Sats. only.
Llangonoyd	8 38	1034		1 5		3 56		....		6 26	7 14			9 24		
Tondu *(above)*	8 48	1044	1250	1 14		4 6		6 13		6 36	7 21			9 34		
Bridgend 56, 60 ....arr.	8 54	1050	1256	1 20		4 12		6 19		6 42	....			9 40		

* Under ½ mile to Maesteg Station, Port Talbot. ‡ Station for Glyncorrwg (2¼ miles).

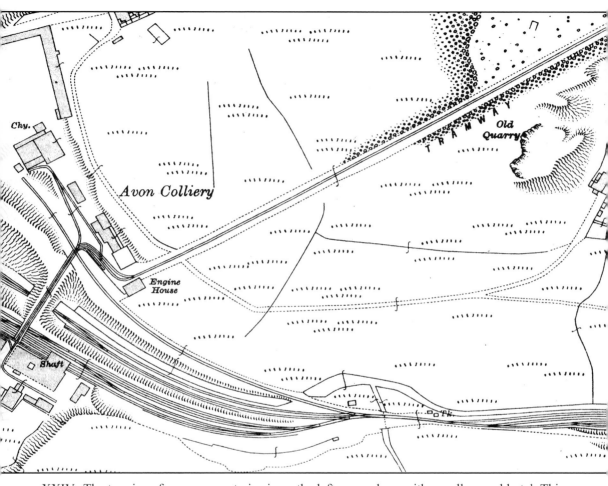

XXIV. The terminus for passenger trains is on the left page, along with a well named hotel. This 1919 edition includes Avon Colliery (1880-1969) and the start of the sidings of Avonmouth Colliery (c1902-12) on the right. The inclined footpath is shown to have a sharp bend in it. The siding for local goods is to the right of the O of ROAD.

PORT TALBOT and BLAENGARW (3rd class only).

Up. — Week Days only.

Miles	Central Station	mrn	mrn	aft S	aft	aft	aft	aft	aft	aft E	aft S	aft S
	Port Talbot ....dep.	7 40	9 25	1 0	1 25	4 35	5 0	7 10	8 45	9 45	10 10	10 40
4	Bryn	7 55	9 40	1 15	1 40	4 50	5 15	7 25	9 0	10 2	10 26	10 56
8½	Maesteg D 78	8 3	9 50	1 23	1 51	5 1	5 23	7 37	9 10	10 10	10.6	11 4
10	Cwmdu		9 55		1 56	5 6		7 42	....	....	10 41	....
12	Lletty Brongu		10 0		2 1	5 11		7 47	....			
13½	Bettws (Llangeinor)		10 6		2 8	5 18		7 54				
15	Pontyrhyll (above)		10 10		2 12	5 22		7 58	....	11 0		
16½	Pontycymmer		10 15		2 17	5 27		8 3		11 5		
17½	Blaengarw ....arr.		10 18		2 20	5 30		8 6		11 8		

Down. — Week Days only.

Miles		mrn	mrn	aft	aft	aft S	aft	aft	aft	aft	aft S	aft S
	Blaengarw ....dep.		10 25		2 30		5 40	8 20				11 20
1	Pontycymmer		10 29		2 34		5 44	8 24				11 25
2½	Pontyrhyll		10 34		2 39		5 49	8 29				11 30
4	Bettws (Llangeinor)		10 38		2 43		5 53	8 33				
5½	Lletty Brongu		10 44		2 50		6 0	8 40				
7½	Cwmdu		10 49		2 55		6 5	8 45				11 46
9	Maesteg D 78	8 15	10 55	1 30	3 15	3 0	6 11	8 51	9 15	11 10	11 52	
13½	Bryn	8 27	11 8	1 43	3 1	4 5	4 36	6 24	9 4	9 28	11 20	12 0
17½	Port Talbot (Cen.) 62 .....arr.	8 40	11 20	1 55	3 26	5 55	6 36	9 16	9 40			

D Neath Road ; under ½ mile to Castle Street Station.   E Except Saturdays.   S Saturdays only.

July 1929

87.   The signal box shown on the map closed on 16th December 1945 and was replaced by this one, which had a 17-lever frame. This eastward view is from November 1957 and features the runround loop. There was a staff of seven in 1930-35. (R.M.Casserley)

88.   No. 7753 is leaving on 2nd August 1958 and from left to right is the school, the hotel, Avon Colliery and the gated private siding to it. The steep footpath can be seen above the coaches. (G.Adams/M.J.Stretton coll.)

89.   It is 22nd August 1959 and 2-6-2T no. 5534 will soon propel its coaches back to Bridgend, once 0-6-0PT no. 8710 has taken its empties onto the colliery line. The station and the signal box were closed on 13th June 1960 and all traffic ceased on 29th September 1969. (S.P.Derek)

Abergwnfi	1903	1913	1923	1933
Passenger tickets issued	30837	36309	46473	32510
Season tickets issued	*	*	132	312
Parcels forwarded	7212	9407	11335	10194
General goods forwarded (tons)	294	318	224	66
Coal and coke received (tons)	19	151	386	516
Other minerals received (tons)	1747	562	1068	186
General goods received (tons)	2855	2392	6956	2704
Coal and coke handled	30795	1055	130351	36921
Trucks of livestock handled	56	91	71	35

August 1939 — LLANTRISANT and PENYGRAIG (One class only).

	Down.	mrn	mrn	mrn		mrn		aft	aft		aft	aft		aft	aft		aft	b	b		
Miles	**Week Days only.**																				
	Llantrisant ....dep.	6 50	8 18	9 23	..	10 55	..	12 50	1 33	..	2 20	7 0	4 10	6 5	..	7 55	9 37	1035	..	..
4	Coed Ely	6 59	8 26	9 32	..	11 3	..	12 58	1 41	..	2 28	7 8	4 18	6 13	..	8 3	9 45	1043	..	..
5	Tonyrefail	7 5	8 34	9 36	..	11 9	..	1 3	1 46	..	2 33	7 13	4 23	6 18	..	8 8	9 50	1048	..	..
7¼	Penygraig ....arr	7 11	8 43	9 44	..	11 18	..	1 11	1 54	..	2 41	7 21	4 31	6 26	..	8 16	9 58	1056	..	..

	Up.	mrn	mrn	mrn		aft	aft		aft	aft		aft	aft		b	S		
Miles	**Week Days only.**																	
	Penygraig ....dep.	7 40	10 0	10 50	..	12 20	1 12	..	1 55	3 23	..	4 55	6 55	8 48	..	9 59	1110	..
2¼	Tonyrefail	7 45	10 5	10 55	..	12 25	1 17	..	1 59	3 28	..	5 0	7 0	8 53	..	10 4	1116	..
3¼	Coed Ely	7 48	10 8	10 58	..	12 28	1 20	..	2 3	3 31	..	5 3	7 3	8 56	..	10 7	1119	..
7¼	Llantrisant 64, 69, 83 ...arr.	7 56	10 16	11 6	..	12 36	1 28	..	2 10	3 39	..	5 11	7 11	9 4	..	1015	1127	..

A Adjoins Penarth Dock Sta   A Except 12th, 19th, and 26th Aug.   a On 17th and 24th Sept.   B Sats. only. Not after 9th Sept.   b Thurs. & Sats.   C or Ƈ General Station   D or Đ Queen St   E, E, or Ɇ Except Saturdays   F To Penarth, p 87   H Mons., Thurs., and Sats.   J or J Not after 10th Sept.   K Wednesdays and Saturdays   L Sats. only, 15th July to 2nd Sept.   Thro' Train to and from Llandrindod Wells, one class only, pages 84, 77, 150, 492, and 493   M One class only   N Not after 27th Aug.   O On 12th, 19th, and 26th August.   Thro' Train to Birmingham (S.H.) page 125a   P From Penarth, page 87   R Except Sats., daily commencing 16th Sept.   S, S, or S Sats only   Ss Stops Sats only   T On 5th, 12th, 19th, and 26th August.   Thro' Train from Birmingham page 122   V Except Mons, Workmen's Train   Ꝡ Not after 8th Sept.   X or X Not after 9th Sept.   Ꝡ Queen St. Not after 10th Sept.   Z Via Penarth, page 87   Ƶ Commences 11th Sept.   ¶ To and from Bridgend, page 88

0502 2nd - SINGLE   SINGLE - 2nd 0502
Abergwynfi to
Abergwynfi   Abergwynfi
Troedyrhiew Garth Troedyrhiew Garth
TROEDYRHIEW GARTH
(W)   1/2 Fare 1/2   (W)
For conditions see over   For conditions see over

601 2nd - SINGLE   SINGLE - 2nd 601
Llangynwyd to
Llangynwyd   Llangynwyd
Abergwynfi   Abergwynfi
ABERGWYNFI
(W)   1/4   1/4   (W)
For conditions see o   conditions see over

7. North of Cymmer
CYMMER CORRWG

90.   The suffix Corrwg was used from 17th September 1926. Part of the platform has been seen in picture 80 and this helps to set the location of this view from 28th September 1951. No. 9737 is working a transfer goods from the ex-GWR route to the Glyncorrwg line. (W.A.Camwell/SLS coll.)

Miles	HOUR→	am		Week Days only							pm	Miles	HOUR→	am					Week Days only					pm
		6	8	11	12	1	3	6	8	10 S	11			6	7	7	8	9	12 S	12	2	4	6	7	9
—	**Bridgend ¶** .. .. dep	45	50	25		45	38	54	15	10	..	25	10		**Abergwynfi** .. .. dep	..	..	45	20	45	..	40	..	33	52	30	15	10
3	Tondu	55	57	33		54	46	1	22	17	..	33	18	2¾	Cymmer (Afan) .. dep	..	35	51	25	50	..	45	..	40	58	35	21	15
6¼	Llangynwyd	..	3	5	41	5	54	9	30	25	..	41	26	3¾	Caerau	..	38	55	29	55	..	50	..	44	2	38	24	20
7	Troedyrhiew Garth ..	..	6	8	44	8	57	12	33	28	..	45	30	4¾	Nantyffyllon	..	42	58	34	58	..	53	..	47	5	42	28	23
8¼	**Maesteg (Castle St.)** ..	15	14	49	13	2	20	42	35	..	51	40	5¼	**Maesteg (Castle St.)** ..	..	45	2	39	2	..	58	..	51	12	47	32	27
9¼	Nantyffyllon	..	19	19	54	19		7	25	47	40	..	57	45	7	Troedyrhiew Garth ..	..	48	6	43	6	..	1	..	55	16		35	30
10¼	Caerau	..	24	24	59	25		12	31	53	44	..	3	52	7½	Llangynwyd	..	51	9	46	8	..	..	5	58	19		38	33
11¼	**Cymmer (Afan)**	..	28	28	3	28		16	34	57	49	..	9	57	11	Tondu	..	28	31	28	16	34	57	49	..	8	27	..	47	42
14	**Abergwynfi** .. .. arr	35	36	11	S37	E25	42	5	57	..	18	S10	..	14	**Bridgend ¶** .. .. arr	21	6	24	0	23	..	26	19	..	14	33	..	54	49

May 1960

NANTEWLAETH COLLIERY HALT

91.   Nantewlaeth Colliery sidings came into use on 3rd April 1917 and the halt for miners opened in 1940. It was closed in 1955 and was photographed in July 1959. The sidings were used until February 1966. (R.M.Casserley)

GLYNCORRWG

92.   The station saw passengers only between 1918 and 1930. No. 9617 is propelling a workmans train north on 11th July 1958. There were nine men employed in 1923-38. (H.C.Casserley)

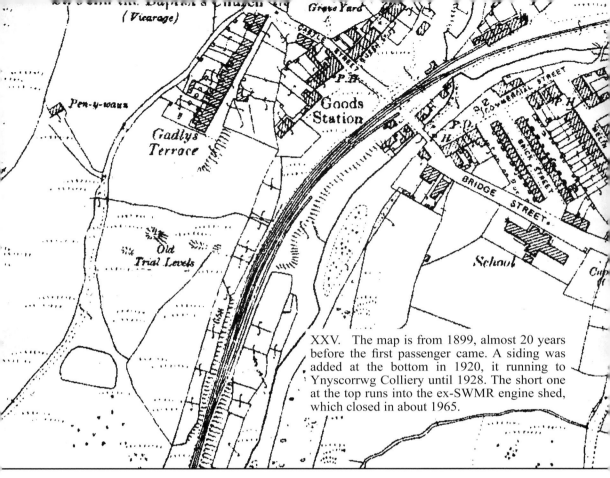

XXV. The map is from 1899, almost 20 years before the first passenger came. A siding was added at the bottom in 1920, it running to Ynyscorrwg Colliery until 1928. The short one at the top runs into the ex-SWMR engine shed, which closed in about 1965.

93. The gates are over Castle Street and the photographer's Hillman 10 is in line with the 1913 signal box, which lasted until September 1968. It is seen on 11th July 1958, along with a lamp with one red glass to warn of the crossing. (H.C.Casserley)

94.   The marshalling yard and goods depot is seen from Castle Street on 13th July 1959, while no. 9736 waits with a load of coal. A miners train stands in the far siding, beyond which was one to Hendregarreg Colliery from 1910-1935. (H.C.Casserley)

NORTH RHONDDA COLLIERY HALT

95.   A railtour reached the end of the line on 2nd July 1960, the year in which the colliery closed. During public service, the halt was known as Blaencorrwg & North Rhondda Platform and was on the other side of the track. The route was in use from 1863 to 1970. (A.M.Davies)

8. East of Port Talbot

PORT TALBOT CENTRAL

96. The last passenger left in 1933 and this is the view 20 years later. Goods continued until 1st June 1960. There were three employees here in 1930-32. The route between here and Maesteg received a direct connection to the new steelworks at Margam on 13th December 1948. The line closed on 31st August 1964. (N.L.Browne/F.Hornby)

XXVI. A small dock was built in 1835-37 by Christopher Talbot to serve the local iron works, copper works and collieries. The PTD&R acquired his creation in 1894 to develop it, as well as the railway links, and retained the family name. Its terminus was opened in 1898 and can be seen on this 1899 map to be very close to the main line station of the GWR. This is illustrated in pictures 82-86 in our *Cardiff to Swansea* album.

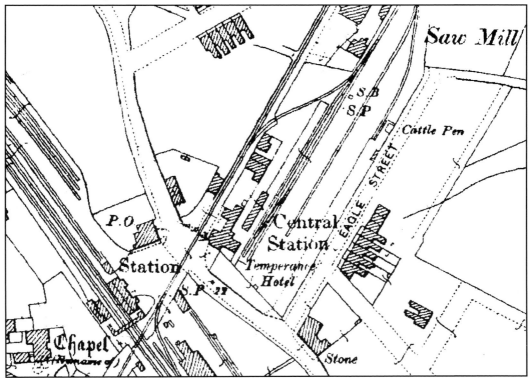

EAST OF PORT TALBOT

97.   Dyffryn No. 2 Box of 1900 controlled the entrance to Dyffryn Yard, where there was a five-road engine shed, plus a two-road carriage shed with three adjacent sidings. Seen on 14th July 1959 is no. 7244, a 7200 class 2-8-2T, a type which was introduced in 1934. The shed was coded 87B by BR. (H.C.Casserley)

98.   The shed was in use from 1896 until March 1964 and at the end of 1947 housed 8 2-8-0Ts, 15 0-6-2Ts and 32 0-6-0PTs. It was photographed in May 1926. The GWR inherited 22 locomotives from the PTR&D. Two more shed roads and the coal stage were provided in 1931. Only one of the latter's locomotives survives: it is an 0-6-0ST of 1901 and is on the Severn Valley Railway, where it carries the GWR no. 813. (GWR)

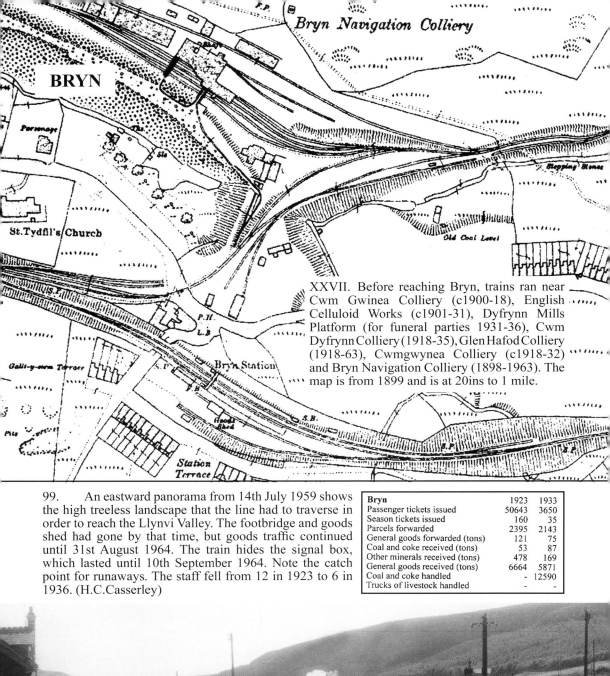

BRYN

Bryn Navigation Colliery

Parsonage

St. Tydfil's Church

Stepping Stones

Old Coal Level

P.H.

L.B.

Galli-y-cwm Terrace

Bryn Station

Pit

Good Shed

Station Terrace

S.B.

XXVII. Before reaching Bryn, trains ran near Cwm Gwinea Colliery (c1900-18), English Celluloid Works (c1901-31), Dyfrynn Mills Platform (for funeral parties 1931-36), Cwm Dyfrynn Colliery (1918-35), Glen Hafod Colliery (1918-63), Cwmgwynea Colliery (c1918-32) and Bryn Navigation Colliery (1898-1963). The map is from 1899 and is at 20ins to 1 mile.

99.   An eastward panorama from 14th July 1959 shows the high treeless landscape that the line had to traverse in order to reach the Llynvi Valley. The footbridge and goods shed had gone by that time, but goods traffic continued until 31st August 1964. The train hides the signal box, which lasted until 10th September 1964. Note the catch point for runaways. The staff fell from 12 in 1923 to 6 in 1936. (H.C.Casserley)

Bryn	1923	1933
Passenger tickets issued	50643	3650
Season tickets issued	160	35
Parcels forwarded	2395	2143
General goods forwarded (tons)	121	75
Coal and coke received (tons)	53	87
Other minerals received (tons)	478	169
General goods received (tons)	6664	5871
Coal and coke handled	-	12590
Trucks of livestock handled	-	-

EAST OF BRYN

100.   The first sidings after leaving Bryn were for Varteg Colliery (1901-27) and then came Bryn Brickworks (1899), seen disused on 29th May 1954. There had been a passing loop here in 1900-39, called West End Tunnel. Next came Cwm Cerwyn Tunnel (1010yds) and then East End Loop (1903-34). Tonhir Colliery (c1903-33) had a siding from it. (P.J.Garland/R.S.Carpenter)

MAESTEG (NEATH ROAD)

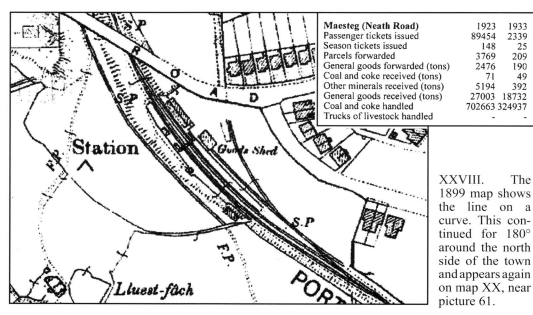

Maesteg (Neath Road)	1923	1933
Passenger tickets issued	89454	2339
Season tickets issued	148	25
Parcels forwarded	3769	209
General goods forwarded (tons)	2476	190
Coal and coke received (tons)	71	49
Other minerals received (tons)	5194	392
General goods received (tons)	27003	18732
Coal and coke handled	702663	324937
Trucks of livestock handled	-	-

XXVIII. The 1899 map shows the line on a curve. This continued for 180° around the north side of the town and appears again on map XX, near picture 61.

101. This northward view is from a postcard from around 1905. Goods traffic continued until 31st August 1964, but the last passenger left on 11th September 1933. The suffix had been added on 1st July 1924. There were 18 employees in 1923 and 11 in 1936. (Lens of Sutton coll.)

102.	No. 5264 is working a train to Cwmdu on 14th July 1959 and largely obscures the signal box, which was in use until 31st August 1964, when the line from Dyffryn Yard was closed. Part of it was then leased to the NCB. (R.M.Casserley)

103.	A panorama from the same day has the former GWR line between Tondu and Maesteg passing under the bridge. (R.M.Casserley)

104.   An SLS tour called on 29th May 1954, hauled by 0-6-0PT no. 3680. The trip started at Bridgend at 1.10pm and ended at Port Talbot General, in time for the 5.53 to London. It will have passed the site of Maesteg Deep Colliery and North's Navigation Colliery sidings. The staff dropped from 7 in 1923 to 3 in 1932, but tons of coal despatched rose from 271,000 to 291,000 tons. (S.Rickard/J&J coll.)

105.   A northward view on 14th July 1959 confirms that there was only one platform, the line on the right being a long reversible loop. The signal box was in use from 19th November 1911 to 31st August 1964. The station opened on 9th June 1913, replacing Garth, which was ½ mile further south. On this section of the route were Cwmdu (St. Johns) Colliery (1910-64) and Bryn Rhyg (1921-33). (R.M.Casserley)

LLETTY BRONGU

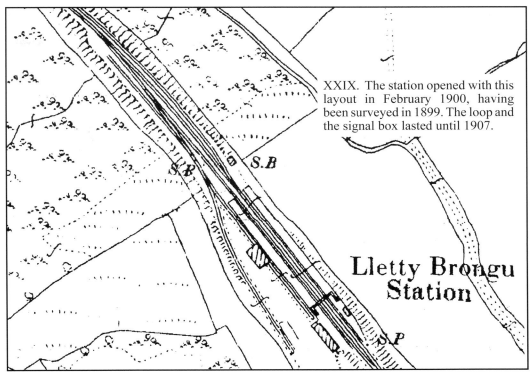

XXIX. The station opened with this layout in February 1900, having been surveyed in 1899. The loop and the signal box lasted until 1907.

S.B

Lletty Brongu Station

106.   The unloved station was recorded in July 1959, the route east to Pontyrhyll having closed in 1949-51. Collieries in the vicinity included Gelli Hir (1905-53), Lletty Brongu (1899-1906), Cwm Cedfyn (1906-28), Celtic Lower (1918-42), Moelgilau (1902-18) and Gwernllyn (c1904-12). The next stop on the route was Bettws Llangeinor. The station opened on 1st January 1900. (R.M.Casserley)

9. Tondu Area

KENFIG HILL

XXX. The route to Porthcawl opened in 1861 and this was the only station between Tondu and the main line at Pyle. The small goods yard was in use until 5th May 1958, when the station closed entirely.

Kenfig Hill	1903	1913	1923	1933
Passenger tickets issued	16004	22114	20084	5021
Season tickets issued	*	*	58	88
Parcels forwarded	3120	10339	11980	12194
General goods forwarded (tons)	39	215	77	6
Coal and coke received (tons)	1102	646	48	17
Other minerals received (tons)	1200	1925	337	-
General goods received (tons)	482	1623	1427	621
Coal and coke handled	-	-	69	56
Trucks of livestock handled	-	-	-	-

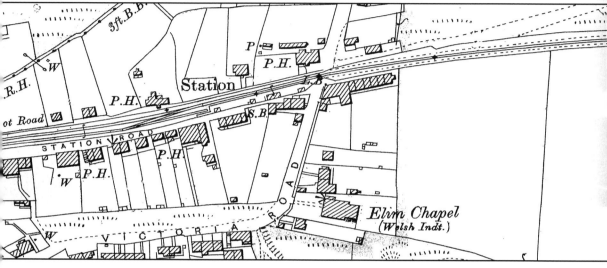

107.   The station opened as Cefn on 1st August 1865 and the name was changed on 1st August 1885. The route was closed on 19th November 1973. Few facilities for gentlemen had ornamental battlements. These are seen on 16th April 1960. The two signals were worked from a ground frame. There was a staff of 14 listed in 1923 and 9 in 1930. (M.Hale)

TONDU

108.   A northward postcard view features the Bridgend platforms and Centre signal box, which was at sometime renamed Middle. South Box was on the Bridgend line from 1901 to 1963.
(Lens of Sutton coll.)

109.   Moving along the up platform, we complete our survey of the east side of the station. There appears to be a supplementary ticket office or possibly a workers pay window.
(Lens of Sutton coll.)

Tondu	1903	1913	1923	1933
Passenger tickets issued	79709	115744	122223	31457
Season tickets issued	*	*	834	162
Parcels forwarded	12239	19825	16123	16700
General goods forwarded (tons)	1379	2458	1264	866
Coal and coke received (tons)	11394	2685	5295	2252
Other minerals received (tons)	7964	5428	2970	2281
General goods received (tons)	6322	9292	7302	2224
Coal and coke handled	155525	99595	226813	132502
Trucks of livestock handled	39	53	70	21

XXXI. The 1921 map is at 6ins to 1 mile and has on the right page our Section 3 top centre, Section 4 top left, the other two lines being freight only. The left page has Section 5 at the bottom, Section 6 at the top and the line to Kenfig Hill and Pyle on the left. Tondu is near the centre. To the right of it is Ogmore Junction, followed by Ynysawdra Junction. South of the town is an industrial complex, which included a wagon works in Tondu Ironworks. The line running south from it served Park Slip Colliery.

110.   The engine shed was completed in 1889 and was in use until February 1964. It was coded by the GWR as TDU and BR applied 86F. There was an allocation of 41 locomotives in 1947, about ten years before this photograph was taken. (Lens of Sutton coll.)

111.   This impressive line up was recorded on 20th April 1958, with nos 7746, 4144, 3627 and 4581 in attendance. (D.K.Jones coll.)

↑ 112. A panorama from the staff allotments on 7th July 1962 has 0-6-0PT no. 9660 arriving with coal from the south and no. 6431 resting between shunts. The Wagon Works was beyond the left border. (S.Rickard/J&J coll.)

113.	Seen on 30th June 1962 is 0-6-0PT no. 9649 running in from Bridgend. The footbridge is seen to join all four platforms. (E.Wilmshurst)

114.	Two views from the footbridge on 7th July 1962 help to complete the survey of the area at its prime. No. 9649 is arriving with a train from Abergwynfi. Beyond the left border was North Box from 1902 to November 1967 and also Coytrahen Park Colliery (1906-1930). (S.Rickard/J&J coll.)

115.   We now look south as the same train leaves for Bridgend. On the right is the washery and coke ovens formerly owned by North's Navigation Colliery. Its sidings are out of view and were closed on 31st May 1963. Evanstown Brickworks, which had a siding from 1911 to 1964, was near the Pyle line. (S.Rickard/J&J coll.)

116.   It is 19th October 1968 and a view from the same position, but slightly to the right, includes a DMU about to leave for Pyle. The line soon becomes single and Velin Vach signal box was at the convergence point until 16th June 1963. The Bridgend line (left) was singled on 22nd October 1967. (J.M.Tulson/F.Hornby coll.)

117.   No. 37220 arrives with coal from Blaengarw on 25th March 1976. The engine shed had been to the left of the wagons (see picture 114). There had been a goods yard, with a 6-ton crane, to the south until 5th April 1965. (T.Heavyside)

118.   Seen on the same day from the same footbridge is no. 37224 running in from the Kenfig Hill direction. The telephone poles on the left are on the side of the station approach road. (T.Heavyside)

119.   One platform was renovated for the 1992 reopening and is seen on 18th October 2002 with no. 143607 in attendance. (P.Jones)

120.   The junction and sole remaining signal box plus the new footbridge were recorded on 13th February 2009. We end with the good news of improving passenger figures. (V.Mitchell)

MP Middleton Press

EVOLVING THE ULTIMATE RAIL ENCYCLOPEDIA

Easebourne Lane, Midhurst, West Sussex.
GU29 9AZ   Tel:01730 813169

www.middletonpress.co.uk   email:info@middletonpress.co.uk
A-978 0 906520 B- 978 1 873793 C- 978 1 901706 D-978 1 904474
E - 978 1 906008   F - 978 1 908174

All titles listed below were in print at time of publication - please check current availability by looking at our website - *www.middletonpress.co.uk* or by requesting a Brochure which includes our *LATEST* RAILWAY TITLES also our TRAMWAY, TROLLEYBUS, MILITARY and WATERWAYS series